HOW TO CHANGE THE WORLD WITH A 501(c)(3)

OLIVIA C. SANTORO

authorHOUSE®

AuthorHouse™ UK
1663 Liberty Drive
Bloomington, IN 47403 USA
www.authorhouse.co.uk
Phone: 0800.197.4150

Published by AuthorHouse 08/22/2017

ISBN: 978-1-5246-8279-8 (sc)
ISBN: 978-1-5246-8278-1 (e)

Library of Congress Control Number: 2017910117

Print information available on the last page.

Any people depicted in stock imagery provided by Thinkstock are models,
and such images are being used for illustrative purposes only.
Certain stock imagery © Thinkstock.

This book is printed on acid-free paper.

CONTENTS

ACKNOWLEDGEMENT

I would like to acknowledge the invaluable counsel, advice, and suggestions of Richard E. Mancuso and Giovanni R. D'Amico of the law firm Whitman Breed Abbott & Morgan LLC, Greenwich, Connecticut with respect to technical and structural issues surrounding 501(c)(3)s.

I would also like to sincerely thank General Robert Magnus, former Assistant Commandant of the United States Marine Corps, for his inspiration and selfless service.

Lastly, I would like to express gratitude to my parents, Charles and Vanessa Santoro, for providing unconditional support and encouragement throughout this process.

DEDICATION

This book is dedicated to the courageous men and women who serve our country and protect our freedoms. 100% of the proceeds from this book will be donated to Mission Critical Veteran Relief Fund to support veterans and their families.

INTRODUCTION

How to Change the World with a 501(c)(3) provides a simple yet comprehensive framework for starting and running a successful 501(c)(3) nonprofit organization. This book is inspired by my experience founding two nonprofits and working with existing nonprofit organizations over the past decade. 501(c)(3) status, which is granted by the IRS to qualified applicants, exempts eligible nonprofits from federal income tax requirements. In certain states, 501(c)(3) status also exempts nonprofits from state corporate income tax obligations. Tax-exempt status allows more of the money donated to worthy and charitable causes to end up supporting those causes directly, and therefore is highly coveted by nonprofits. Additionally, financial contributions made to a 501(c)(3) are deductible by donors for federal income tax purposes, making donating more attractive and lending increased credibility to the organization. The primary audience of this book is individuals who believe passionately in a cause and want to multiply their ability to effect change by utilizing a nonprofit organization. This book will provide you with the tools, confidence, and insight to not only start a 501(c)(3) organization, but to run it like a business in order to maximize its impact on the community.

Note: This book is designed to get you started with a formal 501(c)(3) organization, which involves applying for tax-exempt status from the IRS and satisfying certain maintenance obligations. However, if you are looking to start small or experiment with a charitable organization that collects less than $5,000 per year in gross receipts from public donations, there is an exception to the IRS's filing requirements for this type of small entity, and you do not need for apply to the IRS for formal registration in order to receive many of the benefits of a 501(c)(3) entity. If that is your situation, I believe you will still find this book motivating and informative to get you started, leaving you prepared to expand your organization when the time is right.

Starting and managing a nonprofit can be an extremely gratifying and exciting endeavor, which is why so many of these entities are formed annually. According to the National Center for Charitable Statistics, there are over 1.5 million nonprofits in the United States, with thousands of new organizations being created each year. Organizations serving similar needs or causes may compete in some respects for the donations and attention of their communities and the general public, but as the number of charitable organizations in the United States has grown, so too has interest in supporting and contributing to the causes represented by these organizations. You have likely picked up this book because you are considering starting one of your own; however, there is something to be said for learning to walk before you run. To get a sense of the day-to-day responsibilities of contributing to and managing a nonprofit, and to supplement your reading of this book, consider volunteering at any existing nonprofit and trying to gain exposure to critical tasks such as fundraising. Once you feel that you are ready, this book will guide you through the process of forming your own organization and will lay out the road ahead. I recommend reading the entire book before initiating your planning process, and then re-reading each chapter at the right stage to remind yourself of useful strategies and address any concerns specific to your current state of progress.

Disclaimer: In conjunction with this book, you will need to refer to experienced professionals such as a qualified attorney and accountant who are licensed to practice in your state to ensure that you are fully compliant with local, state and federal requirements and laws. This book has been prepared as a general guide and informational resource for starting and effectively managing a 501(c)(3) organization. It is not intended for use as an authority of legal, tax, or accounting advice. Tax law and the environment in which your organization will operate is always changing, so this book cannot guarantee that the information provided will be advisable or applicable to your specific situation, nor can it guarantee the successful registration and operation of your organization.

Force Multiplier Effect: Starting a 501(c)(3) results in a dramatic "Force Multiplier Effect," providing you with the platform to make a profound difference in the community you are serving well beyond your capacity as an individual. We are all limited in the time and money we can give to a cause on a personal basis, but if you can connect tens, hundreds or thousands of people to your cause, you have multiplied your effect to better the lives of countless individuals in a way you could never have achieved on your own. That magnified impact is the Force Multiplier Effect. The Force Multiplier Effect does not stop there, because its initial impact can also create a ripple effect that itself is multiplied many times over by its impact on the lives of donors, volunteers and staff involved in your organization, and those your organization helps. For example, suppose you give money to help fund a child's high school education. In this case, you have helped one child, and perhaps this child will one day be in an economic position to do the same for another child or otherwise contribute or give back to society. While the chain reaction of this single contribution is meaningful, imagine how powerful it would become if you decided to form a nonprofit dedicated to this cause – and instead of educating one child, you educated entire classrooms of children and recruited dozens of volunteers and hundreds of donors. All of these people will be profoundly changed by their involvement, and the Force Multiplier Effect will greatly magnify the downstream impact of your efforts. The Force Multiplier Effect is analogous to the difference between one person using a megaphone to get her ideas across versus starting a television show to convey that message to an audience of millions. For example, from my own personal experience, using a 501(c)(3) organization gave me the credibility to not only collect donations from dozens of people, but to convince a well-established nonprofit to match any money that my organization raised. Instead of donating whatever I could personally afford out of my own pocket to a wounded Marine, my charity was able to raise a much more significant amount of money for his benefit. A 501(c)(3) organization gives you the ability to demonstrate to your donors that you can leverage their donations to accomplish more than you or they could possibly accomplish alone, and this greatly increases the likelihood they will support your cause now and into the future.

Lastly, by forming your own nonprofit, you can inspire others to take up their cause in a bigger way by starting their own 501(c)(3) organization. This is the broadest impact of the Force Multiplier Effect. No one charity can address the endless needs of society, but by motivating others to pursue their causes through the use of tax-exempt entities, you can multiply your impact on the social good. Ultimately, that is my goal. By sharing my story with you, I hope to do just that.

My experience: I began working with charitable organizations in the wake of Hurricane Katrina, when I was fourteen years old. The first image I saw on the news out of New Orleans was an aerial view of a mother holding a child on the rooftop of their house, reaching upward for help from the helicopter filming them. I never learned if this particular mother and child were rescued, but we all know too well that aid would not come in time to save over 1,800 desperate Louisianans and Mississippians from Katrina's indiscriminate and devastating force. An American cultural icon, the City of New Orleans, was sinking before my eyes, its forlorn population, seemingly on its own, meshing together underneath the crumbling city. Like all Americans, I waited, watched and prayed that government aid would rescue the city and its people; however, news of relief was slow to come. I found myself amazed at the individual stories of ordinary people from across the country responding in countless ways to do whatever was within their means to help. It soon occurred to me that I too could be part of the solution.

Miles and miles from New Orleans, I thought that the best role I could play would be to help finance the rescue and relief efforts. I saw potential donors all around me, and yet with no prior fundraising experience, I was unsure how to proceed. I began gathering an extensive list of people and organizations from whom I could raise money. I was nervous about calling people I did not know personally, and my initial effort was spontaneous and poorly organized. Some people asked me detailed questions regarding the use of funds, but at that point I really did not know how I was going to deploy the money I was raising. Soon, however, I was better able to conceptualize and communicate my purpose and how I was going to achieve it. With growing confidence, my solicitation tactics matured. I did not know this at the time, but the skills I was learning through this experience would guide me in future endeavors.

In order to expedite the relief that this money could bring, I funneled all of it through the Greenwich, Connecticut chapter of the American Red Cross. I felt extremely gratified, with results that surpassed even my wildest hopes for this initiative and a commendation from the President of the local American Red Cross. I became distressed to learn, however, that the Red Cross itself was slow in organizing its own efforts and dispersing funds received. Perhaps a blessing in disguise, I learned how even the best charitable intentions can be hindered by unpreparedness and disorganization, no matter how small or large the purpose or the organization. I wanted to ensure that my future efforts to help those in need were channeled effectively to specific causes and not squandered because of poor planning or mismanagement. My personal Katrina experience, far from the flood waters, taught me that my particular interest was focusing on highly targeted and hands-on charitable pursuits that make a large difference to a smaller number of people. I imagined my organization being a type of surgical strike force in the charitable world. From that inspiration, I founded The Student Relief Fund of Greenwich in September of 2005 and qualified that entity as a 501(c)(3) later that year. The legal status of the Student Relief Fund of Greenwich as a charitable entity gave me the credibility and legal basis I needed to actively solicit contributions tax-free, and to target distributions to hand-picked charitable causes.

It did not take long for the next opportunity to present itself. A family friend informed me of a Sergeant in the U.S. Marine Corps who had been horribly injured by a roadside bomb in Iraq. He was the only surviving member of his seven-person squad and had lost two legs and one arm in the assault. Initially paralyzed from the neck down, the young father had little prospect for ever being able to live together as a family with his wife and their two sons. His condition would require major renovations to his home to accommodate his injuries, which he simply could not afford. I was elated when I learned that some money was being raised to make the needed renovations, but my elation turned to shock when I learned further that even with the renovations, he could not move back into his own home because he had no affordable way of being transported to the doctors and facilities he would need to visit regularly for treatment. His condition required a specially modified transport van with a lift that could provide mobility for his frequent medical transportation needs. I was personally introduced to this proud family, desperate to have their patriot back home, and I was both saddened and energized by their everyday struggles. In the emotion of the moment, I immediately committed to them that I would raise the funds they needed to not only help renovate their home but purchase the van. I did not know how I would do it. I had no plan and had just spontaneously taken on an enormous responsibility.

Using my prior fundraising experience as a stepping stone, I poured my passion into each phone call and refused to take no for an answer. I wrote a brief script for each call and kept a picture of the Sergeant in front of me when I spoke. I arranged to e-mail photos and keep individual donors fully informed of my progress. I also used my tax-exempt organization to form a fundraising partnership with another well-established and interested charity. With my IRS approved entity as my platform, I convinced this charity to match my organization's contribution dollar-for-dollar. Five months later, we proudly presented this marine with a check, enabling him to finally purchase the customized van he so desperately needed.

When the van arrived, I felt that I had come full circle. I had personally overseen the process from the very beginning to the end, and I knew my work had profoundly touched this family. While acquiring a special purpose van required a significant financial commitment, I learned firsthand how important my emotional support was to the entire family, and how my efforts on their behalf gave them comfort in their time of need. Nothing parallels the euphoria I felt that day.

I also realized that I could never have done this on my own. Providing this family with a special purpose vehicle was initially beyond my reach, but through the Force Multiplier Effect I was able to magnify my impact dramatically. Through tax-exempt status, the Student Relief Fund of Greenwich gained credibility within the charitable community, facilitating my partnership with another nonprofit organization, which took my efforts to a whole new level.

The Force Multiplier Effect allows passionate individuals like you and me to achieve so much more than we possibly could through our own hands-on charitable and volunteer efforts. I was amazed at how far my reach extended just by channeling my efforts through a 501(c)(3) entity. Ironically, while I had achieved my goal of providing this family with my support, compassion, and a gift of true mobility, I received far more from this experience than I had given. I learned how to remove myself from my immediate day-to-day affairs and see myself instead as part of something larger. The humility I felt carries with me to this day. Helping those in need through the Student Relief Fund of Greenwich had shown me a great deal about who I am and my life direction.

The Sergeant's resilience and spirit to live deeply inspired me, and I know that the emotional support he received from his community and volunteers was an important factor in his physical and mental recovery. I decided that I wanted to continue working with courageous men and women like him, so I contacted the Assistant Commandant of the Marine Corps at the time, General Robert Magnus, and volunteered to meet with injured Marines at Bethesda Naval Hospital. During my time at Bethesda, I accompanied General Magnus to the hospital rooms of many injured Marines. He presented Purple Hearts and other awards and I spent time talking to each patient. I was utterly numbed each time I opened a new door. The injuries were horrific and in some cases indescribable. Each Marine I met that day had been physically crippled in a life-changing way. Their minds and souls, however, remained intact – searching for a new life's purpose and direction. My sorrow for these men and women turned into admiration, and ultimately, an indelible inspiration. To give back in some way to those who had risked their lives to protect and serve our country left me fulfilled beyond words. After carefully deciding on a new statement of purpose, I decided to start a second 501(c)(3) dedicated to raising funds for families of veterans and law enforcement officers who have been killed or injured while on active duty. That entity is called Mission Critical Veteran Relief Fund.

I have learned that charity takes many forms. While financial aid can alleviate hardship, emotional support is just as important and is often what is needed to create lasting solutions. The most effective approach for providing charitable relief depends on circumstances and is never formulaic. With the self-confidence to set challenging and worthy goals without fear of failure, I enthusiastically look forward to continuing to give back to my community and those in need throughout my life and hope to empower you and your organization with the tools to do the same.

If you are deeply passionate about starting a charitable organization but don't know where to start, this book is for you. While there is a plethora of existing charities to which you can contribute, starting your own charitable entity allows you to take advantage of the Force Multiplier Effect to create a much bigger impact. It allows you to harness the power of others in the form of donors, volunteers and other charities, to multiply your efforts many times over. Through your own charitable entity, you can also ensure that you have control over exactly where donations are going and how they are being used. You will find that 501(c)(3) status will bring with it credibility that will open doors and allow you to form long-lasting personal relationships with your donors, volunteers, beneficiaries and other tax-exempt organizations. You can put in tireless hours as a volunteer, or donate money to a cause and move on, or you can employ the Force Multiplier Effect to magnify your efforts to accomplish so much more and at the same time reap an even greater sense of personal satisfaction and connection that comes with advancing your charitable passion.

CHAPTER 1

HISTORY AND PURPOSE OF 501(c)(3) ORGANIZATIONS

"Americans of all ages, conditions, and dispositions constantly unite together. Not only do they have commercial and industrial associations to which all belong but also a thousand other kinds, religious, moral, serious … I have frequently admired the endless skill with which the inhabitants of the United States manage to set a common aim to the efforts of a great number of men and to persuade them to pursue it voluntarily." – Alexis de Tocqueville, French diplomat and political scientist, 1831[1]

We live in an era of globalization, but I still believe in the power of individuals to make a difference in the world. Tocqueville was right when he identified Americans as possessing a unique gift to harness our ideals to the spirit of volunteerism for the betterment of our society. Let's face it: we as a people are just good at it and we have immeasurably

---

[1] Tocqueville, Alexis de (2003). *Democracy in America*. London: Penguin Books.

advanced our society through countless cooperative efforts, not for money or personal gain, but for the good of our neighbor, the good of our community, and time and time again, to improve the lives of people we will never meet but who need our help. Charity is so important and fundamental to American society that it is one of the short-list characteristics that defines who we are and, as I learned from writing this book, it has been that way from the very beginning of the American experience.

The nonprofit sector's humble beginnings and evolution: Throughout the history of the United States, from the founding of the first colonies in the 1600s to the modern era, Americans have joined together for the purpose of helping their neighbors and less fortunate members of society through community-based charity and volunteerism. Colonists and citizens of our fledgling nation sacrificed their time and energy in order to create voluntary associations, such as hospitals, schools, churches, libraries, fire departments, shelters, and administrative organizations, to help individuals in need and to better their communities. In doing so, early Americans laid a framework for the country's nonprofit sector and established a noble tradition of cooperation and community interest that has persisted and evolved over several centuries.

Beginning with the Wilson-Gorman Tariff Act of 1894, Congress has used the U.S. Tax Code to pursue a public policy in support of the nonprofit sector by passing legislation specifically designed to encourage the establishment of charitable organizations. The Wilson-Gorman Tariff Act granted an exemption from corporate tax obligations to nonprofit entities operated for charitable purposes. Following the introduction of the federal income tax in 1913, the federal government introduced an income tax deduction for public contributions to charitable organizations. These two public policy initiatives set the stage for the growth of charitable organizations and represent the foundation of their fiscal existence to this day. Other Revenue Acts further defined the role of charitable organizations in American society by prohibiting private inurement and political activity (i.e. lobbying), imposing procedural steps for nonprofit entities and revising corporate tax law to allow for deductible corporate contributions.[2]

The concept of what we commonly refer to today as 501(c) organizations stems out of the Revenue Act of 1954, which overhauled the previous half-century of tax law and introduced the modern tax code, including Internal Revenue Code Section 501(c) for tax-exempt organizations. Section 501(c) provides for the various subcategories of nonprofit organizations we are familiar with today. Below I look at Section 501(c) and the types of nonprofit organizations that Congress has determined should be encouraged as a matter of public policy, with a focus on the 501(c)(3) exemption that you can use to greatly expand your charitable impact in the tradition of the best of the American ideals.

---

[2] Arnsberger, P., Ludlum, M., Riley, M., & Stanton, M. A History of the Tax-Exempt Sector: An SOI Perspective. *Statistics of Income Bulletin*, Winter 2008. Retrieved from https://www.irs.gov/pub/irs-soi/tehistory.pdf.

Section 501(c)(3): This Section of the Code provides exemption from federal income tax to organizations that are created and operated exclusively for a purpose that is charitable, religious, scientific, literary or educational, or for the purpose of testing for public safety, fostering national or international amateur sports competition, or preventing cruelty to children or animals. The average person would generally consider each of these purposes to be good and worthy, but some may wonder why tax dollars are sacrificed to advance these causes. Congress has identified six public policy reasons for granting such organizations tax-exempt status: (1) charitable organizations serve the public and therefore should be supported through the provision of tax benefits; (2) charitable organizations provide goods and services that otherwise would have to be provided by the government; (3) measuring the net income of all charitable organizations is unreasonably difficult and would further burden the federal government; (4) charitable organizations promote pluralism; (5) charitable organizations are efficient providers of services but are inherently limited in their ability to raise capital compared to for-profit entities; and (6) organizations that prove their worth through sustained public donation should be afforded special exemption and tax treatment.[3] Thus, if your cause qualifies under Section 501(c)(3) for tax-exempt status, you have the full weight of the Internal Revenue Code and decades of public policy behind you in advancing the interests of your charity.

---

[3] Historical Development and Present Law of the Federal Tax Exemption for Charities and Other Tax-Exempt Organizations. *Joint Committee on Taxation*, (2005, April 19). Retrieved from http://www.jct.gov/x-29-05.pdf.

There are two types of 501(c)(3) organizations under the Internal Revenue Code: public charities, which receive the majority of their funding from public sources, and private foundations, which receive the majority of their income from one or several private funding sources (such as a family trust) and certain investment returns. These two subcategories of 501(c)(3) organizations are subject to different application and maintenance requirements by the IRS.[4] This book will focus on the idea of the public charity, because I believe that it best unleashes the potential of the Force Multiplier Effect by allowing for the involvement of the greatest number of people across all socio-economic levels, representing a truly collective effort. These entities, which inherently rely upon the input and effort of a community on a massive scale, are also limitlessly rewarding and have the most potential to affect the hearts and minds of the general public. For this reason, public charities have exploded in popularity and influence in recent decades and can serve as your ideal vehicle to help create a better world.

Public charity statistics and historical data: Now is a unique and opportune time in American history to start your public charity. According to the IRS, as of the mid-2000s, 501(c)(3) public charities held more than $2 trillion in assets and reported nearly $1.2 trillion in annual revenue. The number of active, tax-exempted public charities increased from

---

[4] Section 501(c)(3) Organizations. *Internal Revenue Service.* Retrieved from https://www.irs.gov/publications/p557/ch03.html; EO Operational Requirements: Private Foundations and Public Charities. *Internal Revenue Service.* Retrieved from https://www.irs.gov/charities-non-profits/eo-operational-requirements-private-foundations-and-public-charities.

approximately 335,000 in 1985 to approximately 933,000 in the mid-2000s, and in each year from 1985 to 2004 except for one, the total assets, liabilities, revenue and expenses of these entities increased. In addition, contributions, gifts and grants to 501(c)(3) organizations increased during every year in that twenty-year span.[5] While the Great Recession posed a serious threat to public charities, they have rebounded with vigor and again play a massive role in American and international societies and in economies throughout the world. Americans have always been world leaders in charitable giving, and recent decades show that they are increasingly eager to donate and to volunteer to advance worthy causes. This creates a vast pool of resources for you to tap into in order to form your charity and support your public purpose goals. In following the guidance of this book, you are taking the first steps toward contributing to hundreds of years of history, and indeed, becoming part of an American institution.

Fortunately, our tax code has been designed (and has adapted) to encourage and facilitate our collective efforts. In fact, it has never been easier to form a new public charity in a world that has never needed it more. In July of 2014, the IRS introduced a simplified form for new nonprofits that meet certain requirements – chiefly, those entities projecting annual gross receipts of $50,000 or less in contributions and total assets of $250,000 or less. The goal was to streamline the review process for the IRS through simplified filing forms

---

[5] Arnsberger, P., Ludlum, M., Riley, M., & Stanton, M. "A History of the Tax-Exempt Sector: An SOI Perspective." Statistics of Income Bulletin, Winter 2008. Retrieved from https://www.irs.gov/pub/irs-soi/tehistory.pdf.

and to encourage the formation of new charities by removing the complexity and reducing the cost of the application process. The new rules have been tremendously successful and have resulted in a reduction in application review time to 30 days or less and a 95% approval rate for new applications.[6] In July of 2016, the IRS lowered the application fee under the simplified form from $400 to $275, further encouraging the formation of new charities.

With these reforms in the law, now is the perfect time for you to pursue your passion for helping others and to join the longstanding tradition of nonprofit leadership that has helped to educate, inspire, and improve the lives of the less fortunate among us. While the process is now easier than ever before, it will still take dedication and determination as you move from being a donor or volunteer – affecting one life at a time – to leading a group effort and a formal organization through which you can reach and improve entire communities in the spirit of the earliest Americans.

Other 501(c) Sections: While 501(c)(3) public charity organizations are probably the most widely known of the 501(c) entities, they certainly do not cover the entire scope of Congress' efforts to promote the public good. There are 29 types of entities permitted under Section 501(c) that qualify

---

[6] Nevius, A.M. (2016, March 1). Form 1023-EZ: First-Year Results Are In. *Journal of Accountancy*. Retrieved from http://www.journalofaccountancy.com/issues/2016/mar/irs-form-1023-ez.html; Gilmer, J. (2015, April 6), How Effective is IRS Form 1023-EZ? A Look at the Numbers. *Harbor Compliance*. Retrieved from https://www.harborcompliance.com/blog/2015/04/06/how-effective-is-irs-form-1023-ez-a-look-at-the-numbers.

for tax-exempt treatment on the donations and contributions that they receive. Of those, a small number also share the highly coveted characteristic of allowing donors to deduct contributions from their income for tax reporting purposes, a hallmark of the success of the 501(c)(3) approach. Below is a list of the other 28 types of 501(c) organizations:

<u>Tax-exempt entities to which contributions are donor-deductible</u>:

- 501(c)(1): Corporations organized by an Act of Congress (including Federal Credit Unions)
- 501(c)(8): Fraternal Beneficiary Societies and Associations
- 501(c)(10): Domestic Fraternal Societies and Associations
- 501(c)(13): Cemetery Companies

<u>Tax-exempt entities to which contributions are not donor-deductible</u>:

- 501(c)(2): Title Holding Corporations for Exempt Organizations
- 501(c)(4): Civic Leagues, Social Welfare Organizations, and Local Associations of Employees
- 501(c)(5): Labor, Agricultural, and Horticultural Organizations
- 501(c)(6): Business Leagues, Chambers of Commerce, and Real Estate Boards
- 501(c)(7): Social and Recreational Clubs
- 501(c)(9): Voluntary Employees Beneficiary Associations

- 501(c)(11): Teachers' Retirement Fund Associations
- 501(c)(12): Benevolent Life Insurance Associations, Mutual Ditch or Irrigation Companies, and Mutual or Cooperative Telephone Companies
- 501(c)(14): State-Chartered Credit Unions, Mutual Reserve Funds
- 501(c)(15): Mutual Insurance Companies or Associations
- 501(c)(16): Cooperative Organizations to Finance Crop Operations
- 501(c)(17): Supplemental Unemployment Benefit Trusts
- 501(c)(18): Employee-Funded Pension Trusts created before June 25, 1959
- 501(c)(19): Post or Organization of Past or Present Members of the Armed Forces
- 501(c)(21): Black Lung Benefit Trusts
- 501(c)(22): Withdrawal Liability Payment Fund
- 501(c)(23): Veterans' Organization (created before 1880)
- 501(c)(25): Title Holding Corporations or Trusts with Multiple Parent Corporations
- 501(c)(26): State-Sponsored Organizations Providing Health Care Coverage for High-Risk Individuals
- 501(c)(27): State-Sponsored Workers' Compensation Reinsurance Organizations
- 501(c)(28): National Railroad Retirement Investment Trust

- 501(c)(29): Co-Op Health Insurance Issuers[7]

Congress has eliminated certain previously approved types of tax-exempt entities. The 501(c)(20) exemption for Qualified Group Legal Services Plans was eliminated in 1992, and the 501(c)(24) exemption for Single-Employer Benefit Trusts was eliminated in 2006.[8]

---

[7] Publication 557 (Rev. January 2017): Tax-Exempt Status for Your Organization. Internal Revenue Service. Retrieved from https://www.irs.gov/pub/irs-pdf/p557.pdf.

[8] 501(c)(20). *Ballotpedia*. Retrieved from https://ballotpedia.org/501(c)(20); 501(c)(24). *Ballotpedia*. Retrieved from https://ballotpedia.org/501(c)(24).

CHAPTER 2

FIRST STEPS

Harnessing your passion to find your purpose: The first and most important step of starting a 501(c)(3) is determining your charity's purpose, which requires extensive research and soul-searching. This takes place before you begin your application process for tax-exempt status. When considering your mission, ask yourself if this cause is something you are capable of being passionate about in the long run and if it will resonate strongly with potential funders. Your passion must be contagious if you hope to motivate others to give their money, time, and energy in pursuit of your purpose. It is your job to make sure others become just as invigorated about the focus of your cause as you are. Having passion for your mission is critical; however, remember that a nonprofit is very much like a business, and you need to do your homework before starting one.

Conduct research to ensure there is a need for your 501(c)(3): There must be a demonstrated need for a new nonprofit in the community you aim to serve in order for you to successfully fundraise. There are many ways to assess the needs of a particular community. Consider interviewing leaders in the community or conducting surveys (via phone, mail, or in person) to better understand the extent of the need. Determine if there are existing nonprofits with a similar agenda in your region. If so, your organization may be redundant, which will only increase the competition for limited resources. If this is the case, rather than starting your own organization, consider getting involved with existing charities in your interest area. You can donate, volunteer, join their staff, or inquire about joining their Board of Directors. This does not mean you will be giving up on starting your own 501(c)(3) organization, but rather, this can be a stepping stone to gain experience and an opportunity to identify a different way to serve your cause that may not be served by the existing charities. When you do decide to start a 501(c)(3), lay out how your nonprofit will be different or better than others. Research the root causes of the problem or problems you are trying to solve and work backwards from there. It is important to make sure your charitable entity addresses problems head-on rather than acting as just a "band-aid." The objective is to make a lasting, positive impact on the lives of others.

Mission statement: Once you have identified the purpose of your charity, distill it into one or two succinct sentences; longer than this, and your purpose is not clear enough. This is your *mission statement*, which should clearly and persuasively communicate your purpose to others. Internally, your mission statement should motivate and unite your board members, staff, and volunteers around a single cause. Externally, your mission statement should inspire potential funders, partners, and collaborators to work with you. Importantly, if you apply for 501(c)(3) status, the IRS may use your mission statement to assess whether your organization meets its requirements. The strongest mission statements are clear, short, and easy to remember. Keep it simple! Think of your mission statement as your organization's slogan – one of its most powerful public relations tools. According to topnonprofits.com, the average mission statement length for the top 50 nonprofits is 15.3 words.[9] Studying examples of successful mission statements can be helpful. Here are a few from my favorite organizations:

- *TED:* Spreading ideas. (2 words)
- *The Humane Society:* Celebrating Animals, Confronting Cruelty. (4 words)
- *Wounded Warrior Project:* To honor and empower wounded warriors. (6 words)
- *National Parks Conservation Association:* To protect and enhance America's National Park System for present and future generations. (13 words)
- *Cleveland Clinic:* To provide better care of the sick, investigation into their problems, and further education of those who serve. (18 words)
- *The U.S. Fund for UNICEF*: We work for the survival, protection and development of children worldwide through fundraising, advocacy and education. (16 words)
- *Teach for America*: Our mission is to enlist, develop, and mobilize as many as possible of our

---

[9] Topnonprofits.com. Top 50 nonprofits based on a series of web, social, and financial metrics.

nation's most promising future leaders to grow and strengthen the movement for educational equity and excellence. (30 words)

- *Make-A-Wish:* To grant the wishes of children with life-threatening medical conditions to enrich the human experience with hope, strength and joy. (21 words)

If you strongly feel that your mission statement must be longer than two sentences, topnonprofits.com recommends creating a supplementary mission tagline (a few words) which is easier for people to remember. This can even be incorporated into your logo. Despite its short length, writing your mission statement will undoubtedly require multiple revisions. I recommend focus testing your mission statement on friends, relatives, and members of the community you hope to serve to ensure your purpose is coming through clearly. Even after you have successfully started your 501(c)(3), you should review your mission statement frequently. Writing an effective mission statement ultimately lays the groundwork for everything else you wish to communicate about your charity.

Vision statement: In addition to a mission statement, most nonprofits have a supplemental *vision statement*, which is a single compelling sentence describing how the world would be if the organization achieved its most ambitious aspirations on a grand scale. Since your 501(c)(3) is serving others, your vision must be for the community you are helping, not for the organization itself. Start by filling in the blank: "Our vision is a community where ____" and then revise the wording as you see fit. Here are the vision statements for some of the organizations mentioned above:

- *Make-A-Wish:* Our vision is that people everywhere will share the power of a wish. (13 words)
- *Teach for America:* One day, all children in this nation will have the opportunity to attain an excellent education. (16 words)
- *Cleveland Clinic:* Striving to be the world's leader in patient experience, clinical outcomes, research and education. (14 words)

Values statement: While mission and vision statements are common in the nonprofit sector, many organizations do not take the time to write a *values statement.* The values statement represents how an organization chooses to conduct and represent itself both internally and externally. Having a strong values statement ensures that your nonprofit remains honorable in its endeavors, unites your team around a common set of ethics, and guides leadership regarding how and where to direct the organization. Many nonprofits claim a values statement is a waste of time because it has no practical applications; however, this could not be further from the truth. Nonprofit organizations face values-related issues frequently. Here are some examples of common questions that all revolve around an organization's values:

- Who are acceptable partners or sponsors for the organization?

- Are there persons or groups from whom we cannot accept funding?
- What percentage of funds raised can we use for administrative purposes?

Ask yourself what values would need to be present in the community you are serving for your vision statement to become a reality. From there, assess how you can incorporate those same values into your organization's work. What do you want the community to be able to say about the way your organization works? The mission, vision, and values statements complement each other in important ways: The mission statement defines your purpose, the vision statement illustrates how your purpose translates into the future, and the values statement describes how your organization will achieve its ambitions.

Using the three statements in practice: The mission, vision, and values statements are practical tools that guide your organization towards creating a better future for the community you are serving. Start each board and staff meeting by briefly reviewing and recommitting yourselves to these statements in order to set the tone for your discussions and to put your decisions into perspective. This is especially important during annual planning sessions. Ensure that every board member, employee, and volunteer has a hard copy of these statements to guide them in their daily practices. You may even consider framing these statements on your office walls. If you have a website, put these three statements front and center so that potential partners and donors understand your goals and the values and principles for which your organization stands.

CHAPTER 3

IMPLEMENTING YOUR MISSION WITH A BUSINESS PLAN

A business plan is the blueprint for a startup nonprofit's formation, operation, and pursuit of success. It marries an organization's short-term goals with its long-term vision, ultimately providing the credibility to attract funding, partners, and key executives. Management will refer to its business plan regularly to assess whether the organization is on the right course with meeting milestones and goals. While creating a business plan demands a considerable amount of time and energy, and may seem daunting, it is crucial in today's competitive nonprofit environment to have this important information thought through before taking on initiatives. The entire process can be completed in a matter of weeks, contingent on the scope and maturity of your organization. With a thoughtful business plan, you will be equipped to manage your organization professionally and compete for resources.

SWOT analysis: Strong business plans should capitalize on an organization's strengths, mitigate its weaknesses, and strategize the best methods for development. Start the business planning process by evaluating the nonprofit's internal strengths and weaknesses, as well as external opportunities, and threats (this is commonly abbreviated by the acronym SWOT). SWOT analysis is just a starting point, and it is perfectly acceptable if your nonprofit is at too early a stage to allow you to think of many bullet points for each category. The objective is for this analysis to result in a list of ideas that can then be turned into goals and strategies.

A hypothetical SWOT analysis for a startup nonprofit may look something like this:

- *Strengths:*
  - o Easy-to-use website is up and running
  - o Committed and passionate board members
- *Weaknesses:*
  - o Not well known in community
  - o Average donation size is only $20
  - o Very small volunteer base
- *Opportunities:*
  - o One of our new board members has strong relationships with key community leaders and potential donors
  - o Need for our service is growing in the community

- o New Facebook page has the potential to direct more people to our website, which could expand our mailing list
- *Threats:*
  - o New and similar nonprofit was just founded, which will lead to increased competition for funding
  - o Difficult economic environment

The above analysis suggests that poor public awareness is preventing the organization from bringing in volunteers and larger sized donations. Its website, Facebook page, and new board member's strong community ties should be used to spread awareness and attract key donors, which will mitigate the threat of increased competition and the weak economic environment.

Setting S.M.A.R.T. goals: Goals describe what an organization needs to accomplish to fulfill its mission and are the end-result toward which energy and hard work are focused. With strong goals in place, an organization is better able to celebrate its success and demonstrate to funders, partners, staff, and volunteers the ways in which they are making a difference. In his 1981 article entitled "There's a S.M.A.R.T. Way to Write Management's Goals and Objectives," George T. Doran outlined a five-part formula for defining, measuring, and ultimately achieving goals that is now widely used. According to the article, goals should be specific, measurable, achievable, relevant, and timely:

S is for specific: Goals must be well-defined and clear enough to provide proper direction. It is not enough to say, "we want to make more of an impact than last year." That goal is extremely vague and can mean a multitude of different things. Be specific: we want to raise X dollars or recruit X new volunteers; we want to host two effective fundraising events in order to fund these specific outreach or relief efforts.

<u>M is for measurable:</u> By setting quantifiable goals, you can objectively evaluate your success. While some benchmarks will be very clear, such as amount of money raised, others will be more challenging. For example, how do you measure the success of your social media platforms in spreading public awareness? Counting the number of updates and posts your organization writes does not adequately measure readership, but looking at number of website or Facebook page visitors does (see Chapter 8: Digital Marketing Strategy for more information on measuring the success of your social media pages).

<u>A is for ambitious yet achievable:</u> Goals need to be challenging, yet possible. Setting goals that are too difficult can be counterproductive and ultimately discouraging; setting and accomplishing realistic goals will give you momentum and demonstrate that your organization can be successful in each smaller step that it takes.

<u>R is for relevant:</u> Goals should make sense in the context of your organization's mission and vision. Set goals that will appeal to the passions and interests of your leadership and volunteers.

<u>T is for timely:</u> Having a visible deadline is another important aspect of setting specific goals. Timelines provide a sense of

urgency and prevent procrastination. They help members of the organization stay organized and on task.

An example of a S.M.A.R.T. goal:

John works at a nonprofit that provides $5,000 in tragedy assistance to Gold Star families (immediate family members of a fallen member of the U.S. military). He is planning the nonprofit's annual fundraiser and sends the following memo to the organization's internal team:

> *This year's campaign will run from January 10th through January 25th. Our primary goal is to raise $50,000 in donations so that we can provide ten Gold Star families with immediate tragedy relief.*
>
> *Last year, we raised $30,000 and supplied six Gold Star families with financial assistance. While this year's goal may seem aggressive in relation to last year's results, we believe that our recently expanded network of donors and the improved economic environment make it possible.*

John's goal of raising $50,000 in donations is both specific and measurable. While this amount is ambitious relative to last year's results, John explains why it is achievable. The funds will be used to provide $5,000 checks to ten Gold Star families and therefore the goal is relevant to the organization's mission. Furthermore, the deadline of January 25th makes the goal time-bound.

In the nascent stage of your organization, I recommend setting no more than three lofty goals at a time to keep your organization highly targeted in its campaign efforts. Once your goals are established, make sure they remain top of mind and are not forgotten about. Evaluate your progress every couple of months and, once goals have been achieved, set new ones.

Program planning: Nonprofits provide services and ultimately achieve their goals through programs. A program is an ongoing set of resources and activities designed to address an unmet need in the community and should be closely aligned with the organization's mission. The number of programs varies depending on the size and maturity of the organization. While a startup nonprofit may only have one or two programs, a more established organization may have upwards of twenty. No matter how many programs your organization has, it is helpful to simplify the planning process into four principal components. According to the logic model, these components are:[10]

1. Inputs: Various inputs and resources required for the program, such as money, volunteers, staff, and equipment.
2. Activities: How the nonprofit's services are carried out, such as through counselling or building houses.
3. Outputs: The units of service, such as number of people counseled, books donated, or houses constructed.

---

[10] W. K. Kellogg Foundation (2001). W. K. Kellogg Foundation Logic Model Development Guide.

4. <u>Outcomes:</u> Effect on the community receiving the service. For example, children receive emotional support, students are empowered, homeless receive housing. These results are ultimately what keep programs on course.

The chief executive, board members, and relevant staff (if the organization has any) should all be involved in program planning. Furthermore, input from community representatives is an especially critical aspect of the program's marketing process and research. These individuals will provide valuable insight about their community's demographics, needs, and preferences. The more you know about the community, the better equipped you are to help address its needs.

Know your competition: Before starting a new program within your organization, determine who your competitors are. One might think that in the general spirit of giving, nonprofits should work closely with one another and share their proprietary information for the greater good, being completely transparent with other charities; however, keep in mind that nonprofits ultimately compete for the attention, participation, and resources of the community. In that way, even with common goals in mind, nonprofits can be competitors in the same way that two companies in the for-profit business world can share a demographic and processes but prioritize their own interests. Consider the following questions: What organizations are offering similar programs? What community needs are you competing to serve? Is the community large enough to require numerous charitable fronts addressing the same specific cause? What are the similarities and differences between your competitors' program(s) and yours? What are their strengths and weaknesses? How are they doing so far? How do you plan to compete?

Stay within your budget: Determine if the proposed program makes sense in the context of your budget. To minimize overhead costs, avoid developing programs that require heavy recurring administrative expenses. Reflect on your proposed program portfolio and list what resources are necessary to accomplish them. Are your efforts hampered by outdated information technology? Do you need to hire a team with a certain knowledge base or skillset? Is your organization currently too understaffed to take on another program? Project these costs and determine where you will find the money to pay for these added expenses.

Environmental scan: Business plans need to anticipate potential external developments and trends that could impact the organization and address how the nonprofit is equipped to respond. Anticipating these developments and trends will make your organization stronger and more resilient even if planned-for issues never present themselves; preparedness is the key to success. For example, nonprofits that have diversified sources of donations will be better prepared to survive a weak economic environment. Consider the following questions:

- What are the demographic trends in the community and will these trends impact our line of service in any way?

- How is our competitive landscape evolving? How can we carve a niche for ourselves? Should we collaborate with any competing organizations?
- How sustainable is our current funding? Are there any changes in government funding of which we need to be aware? Where can we find potential new sources of funding?
- Are our wages and employees benefits competitive across the nonprofit industry? Do they meet the reasonable expectations of our personnel, and are they reasonable such that they do not inflate our operating expenses?

Determine what your organization can do now to prepare for each potential risk or trend and how it would respond in real time if the situation were to occur. Your *mission* should not have to change in response to external factors, but such factors may require you to adjust the programs and steps taken to achieve your mission.

Start writing: Once you have carefully considered your organization's goals, programs, costs, and key environmental factors, start drafting the business plan. A typical nonprofit business plan outline is structured in the following way, although if your organization is a start-up, you may not have enough information to include all of these sections. In that case, include the information you do have and revise your plan at a later date to make it as comprehensive as possible.

1. Table of Contents

2. <u>Executive summary:</u> Describe the nonprofit and provide a brief overview of the business plan.
   o   Include mission, vision, and values statements.
3. <u>Organizational structure and management team:</u> Explain how your nonprofit is organized and the key personnel leading each department.
4. <u>Market overview and competitive landscape:</u> Discuss trends or recent developments in the community you serve. What nonprofits are similar to yours and how do you differ?
5. <u>Programs, services, products:</u> Describe in detail what programs, services and/or products you currently offer or will eventually launch.
6. <u>Marketing plan:</u> This is usually the largest section of the business plan. Discuss the constituents your nonprofit is targeting for support and explain the specific strategies your organization is employing to reach and elicit donations from them.
7. <u>Financials:</u> Explain the current and projected financial status of your organization. Explain your fundraising plan and list any major support you have received including grants and donations.
   o   Consider including an income statement, balance sheet, cash flow statement, and financial projections. Keep these financials current and updated as your organization grows.
8. <u>Appendix</u>

While the process of writing a detailed plan will provide your organization with a thorough document that has a structural beginning and end, your business plan is never truly "done." Organizations should revisit the business plan frequently to assess what has yet to be accomplished and what changes to the plan need to be made. You will likely find that your work as an individual and volunteer shifts toward management and business-related concerns and away from hands-on volunteerism; by relying on and frequently revisiting your business plan, you can ensure that the organization and its members stay focused on the big picture and the goals you established early on through specific action and well-considered programs.

CHAPTER 4

BOARD OF DIRECTORS

Few things are as important to the success and well-being of your organization as finding the right composition of leaders to serve on your Board of Directors. Board members are ultimately responsible for an organization's decision-making and must guide planning and strategy to ensure that the organization fulfills its mission. While not typically involved in day-to-day operations, board members make key decisions, set policies and strategies, oversee activities and events, and are responsible for the accounting and financial reporting of the organization. Strong board members can serve as the backbone of a nonprofit and provide it with the public credibility it needs to improve its fundraising potential.

Identifying and recruiting board members is an incredibly important yet challenging process. According to Leading with Intent's 2015 report, approximately 60% of nonprofit leaders find recruiting board members difficult.[11] This process is challenging because building a board is more than just about filling seats at the table, or finding individuals interested in adopting a distinguished title or credential for their CV. In reality, finding ideal board members is about recruiting individuals who have skills and viewpoints that align with your organization's purpose, goals, and needs both now and into the future. A Board of Directors should not recognize, give authority to, or rely on one accomplished member, or put a particular member or member's perspective on a pedestal, but should rather be comprised of the right blend of talents, expertise, connections, and perspectives. All board members will share the common interest in addressing a particular public need, but a diversity of perspectives will keep your leadership open-minded and flexible in coming up with solutions to problems and thinking outside of the box.

Recruitment: Before commencing the recruiting process, envision your ideal board member composition. While having a few wealthy members who can make substantial financial contributions may appeal to your organization's financial needs, you must also ensure your board consists of individuals who are willing to work hard and care deeply about the organization's mission. According to Leading with Intent, the most successful boards are carefully assembled with regard to leadership characteristics, communication styles and diversity of perspective and background. Important board member qualities include:

---

[11] Leading with Intent 2015: A National Index of Nonprofit Board Practices, http://leadingwithintent.org

- Honesty: Board members must uphold public trust and embody the nonprofit's character and mission.
- Diversity of background, perspective, and expertise: Strong nonprofit boards understand that diversity is essential to an organization's success, encouraging lively discussions and resulting in innovative solutions. Members must be open-minded, accepting, and willing to work with each other.
- Passion: Every board member must share passion for and dedication to your mission.
- Commitment: Board members should attend most monthly meetings and regularly volunteer for your organization, whether by working alongside rank-and-file volunteers and staff or by giving their time to the organization in other ways (i.e. in using their expertise to address the organization's financials or modify the business plan and reassess the effectiveness of programs as needed). Therefore, select individuals who are capable of and enthusiastic about dedicating their time and contributing to the charity's success. Inactive board members should be removed. Since it is difficult to remove members (for reasons both personal and political), consider stipulating a mechanical removal process for a predetermined number of absences each year, so that attendance and contribution requirements are well-established and consistent for all board members and so that you do not need to make the judgment

call about when to initiate a vote to remove an ineffective board member. An absent or inactive board member – even someone who has made donations in the past, or a board member who is a close friend – can burden the rest of the board by holding a position that might be better occupied by an interested individual willing to sacrifice their time and contribute to your leadership.

- <u>Knowledge about the community and cause:</u> It is beneficial to recruit individuals who understand and have experience in the community you aim to serve and who have particular expertise in your organization's cause. You may be able to identify such individuals in your earliest planning stages, when conducting interviews or networking in the community to assess the public need you aim to address. Keep a list or chart of contacts and do not hesitate to ask prominent figures in the community either whether they are interested in joining your board or whether they have any recommendations for others who may be interested in accepting a leadership position with your nonprofit.

- <u>Financially savvy:</u> A board is responsible for overseeing the organization's budget and financial reporting. It is therefore beneficial to have at least one board member who understands financial accounting.

Create a spreadsheet to help you visualize the characteristics you need to seek out when looking for board members.

When evaluating candidates, check off the skills you believe each person will bring to the board. Avoid candidates who seem motivated by enhancing their reputations without expecting to have to do much work.

Write a board member job description informing prospective members of their roles and responsibilities and create a letter of commitment outlining what is expected of each board member. While this letter is not a legally binding agreement, it does set expectations. This will prevent early resignation of members who did not understand the extent of their required commitments. Be sure to cover key topics such as stipulations for removing a board member, term limits, conflicts of interest, and the board's role in fundraising.[12]

Volunteers often make strong board members because they are passionate about the cause, are hands-on, know how an organization works, and bring a realistic viewpoint to meetings. Donors can also be excellent board members since they have already demonstrated their commitment to the organization and care about its success. Furthermore, major donors usually have strong connections throughout the community and can help bring in other contributions. State and federal laws may restrict compensation of board members, and generally, charities should refrain from compensating board members except to reimburse reasonable expenses incurred in connection with volunteer service. To recruit top talent outside of your current volunteers,

---

[12] Board Composition and Recruitment. *BoardSource*. Retrieved from https://boardsource.org/fundamental-topics-of-nonprofit-board-service/composition-recruitment.

donors, or paid employees, utilize social media and other online platforms to let people know a board position is open. Many professional recruitment websites exist that make it easier to find board candidates and make it easier for board candidates to find you. These include LinkedIn Board Connect, VolunteerMatch, and TapRoot.

The appropriate number of board members is highly dependent on the organization's needs and scope. In most states, statutory law requires that the minimum size for nonprofit boards is three people. While there is no cap on the number of board members an organization can have, advantages and disadvantages of larger boards include:

Advantages:
- Increased diversity of perspectives and expertise
- More available seats for financial and legal advisors or community leaders
- Members can divide and conquer more work
- Fundraising may be more effective because there are more board members with connections to potential donors

Disadvantages:
- Less individual accountability
- Large groups may inhibit effective and interactive discussions
- Some voices may not be heard, which can lead to apathy and loss of interest for those being excluded
- Meetings are more difficult to schedule

Newly formed nonprofits typically start with a small number of board members and expand as the organization and its programs become more established. No matter the size of your board, consider having an odd number of members to avoid stalemates resulting from tie votes.

Orientation: Orientation programs ensure that every new board member operates under the same instructions and receives the same information at the outset of his or her involvement with the organization's leadership. During orientation, each board member should sign the letter of commitment confirming that they understand expectations. Provide a packet of reference materials to help new members get up to speed quickly. These materials may include:

- Board job description
- Mission, vision, and values statements
- Business plan
- Names and contact information of current board members
- Board meeting minutes from last few sessions
- Articles and bylaws of your organization
- Calendar of upcoming events

Compensation: Paying board members in the nonprofit sector is not recommended and can ultimately harm public relations, call into question the organization's financial integrity, and create potential conflicts of interest. The inherent rewards for board members serving nonprofits include enhancing their professional standing, getting to know other influential individuals, developing a sense for community needs, and feeling good about their contribution to society. Some states have rules regarding board compensation, so check your state's laws and consult a local attorney if you are unsure about restrictions on board compensation.

Officers: In order to apply for 501(c)(3) status, the IRS requires your board to appoint officers to hold the positions of President, Secretary, and Treasurer at a minimum. Your state's laws may also require additional officer positions for your nonprofit. Think of the required officer positions as having the following typical responsibilities:

- <u>President:</u> Leads board meetings, appoints committees, guides the organization, and serves as spokesperson for the organization.
- <u>Secretary:</u> Records and maintains the minutes at board meetings and distributes these records to board members.
- <u>Treasurer:</u> Oversees the organization's finances and makes regular financial reports and presentations to the board.

Tenure, sector knowledge, and strong communication skills are common characteristics sought in and useful for a board's leaders. Typically, these individuals are elected to two-year terms by the board, but your bylaws may vary the length of your officers' terms.

Committees: Board committees take on specific responsibilities when the work in question is too nuanced and time-consuming for the entire board to deal with; the ability to delegate effectively rather than force the entire leadership to address every single issue is as important in the nonprofit sector as it is in a for-profit business. Committees should be small enough to remain focused and efficient, but at the same time, large enough to include diverse perspectives and constituencies. Most committees should contain between three and ten people, depending on the importance and scale of the task.

Permanent (also known as "standing") committees typically cover topics such as fundraising, finance, programs, and public relations. Temporary (also known as "ad hoc") committees are formed to deal with shorter-term projects such as special events or executive searches. Both permanent and temporary board committees make regular reports and presentations to the full board regarding their assignments. Some larger boards have an executive committee, which consists of the board's officers. The executive committee sets the agenda for board meetings and comes together on an as-needed basis. Depending on the bylaws of the organization, some executive committees are authorized to make decisions on behalf of the full board. This can be useful during emergencies or in special circumstances. While there are many opportunities to establish committees, the board needs to limit the number of committees to what can realistically be supported and staffed within the organization. The board is not obligated to form committees – committees should be viewed simply as an optional tool to focus the work of the organization.

Getting the most out of your board: Few nonprofit founders are adequately prepared for the politics of working with a board, but this is a critical skill to develop. You will quickly become frustrated and ineffective as a leader if you have weak alliances with your board members. Remember, since board members have other obligations and are not present on a daily basis, they do not understand the business as well as you do. It is your job to inform board members of key trends and occurrences, provide routine data and updates, help them anticipate and interpret important changes, and keep them motivated and committed. Ultimately, a strong relationship with your board is reflected by frequent and effective communication, the board's confidence in you as a credible leader, a common philosophy for handling operational topics, and, above all, mutual respect and trust. The board is ultimately on your team and is central to your work. Collaborate and negotiate with your board to come up with the best solutions for the organization. Taking your relationship with the board seriously is critical for the nonprofit to operate effectively and will reduce conflict in the long-run.

Some board members are not as involved as others and contribute less to the organization. Not all board members will show up to every meeting, read the materials, and participate in fundraising and volunteer activities. While you should be understanding of time constraints and other commitments, do everything you can to maximize each member's participation. Here are some suggestions:

- Write a board member letter of commitment.
  While this document is not legally binding, it
  will make the responsibilities board members
  are expected to fulfill crystal clear. Include such
  topics as board meeting attendance requirements
  and expectations for financial contributions to the
  organization.
- Well in advance of each meeting, send an email
  reminding members of the upcoming date,
  include the upcoming meeting agenda and the
  minutes from the prior meeting.
- Bylaws can state the requirements for board
  participation. For example, you may stipulate that
  a board member may face dismissal by missing
  two consecutive board meetings in a one-year
  period without a legitimate excuse.
- Ensure each board member feels that his or her
  opinion matters. Seek their expertise and advice in
  between board meetings and be sure to recognize
  and show appreciation for their contributions.

The level of a board member's participation reflects his or
her passion and enthusiasm for your cause. The more board
members believe in and are inspired by your mission, the
more involved they are likely to be.

The majority of board work takes place during meetings.
The board president is responsible for making sure these
meetings are well-organized and use members' time
effectively. Frequency of meetings depends on the needs
of the organization – some meet on a monthly basis,

while others meet quarterly, semi-annually or even once a year. The president may call emergency meetings to handle special situations. To start, consider conducting board meetings once per quarter, which is enough to keep members engaged but not so frequent as to make meetings redundant or burdensome. Remember that board members are essentially volunteers, so use their time and resources effectively. To keep meetings as efficient as possible, keep the length under two hours.

Insurance: Protect your board members from legal and financial accountability through directors and officers insurance. Today, many prospective board candidates will ask if you offer such insurance to protect your directors and officers from personal liability for the organization's decisions, especially as those decisions pertain to personnel. See Chapter 12 for details on this type of insurance and other policies that will be beneficial for your organization to consider.

CHAPTER 5

CREATING YOUR LEGAL ENTITY AND FILING FOR TAX-EXEMPT STATUS

Now that you have done your research, identified your organization's mission and values, established your business plan and recruited strong leadership to guide you forward, you are ready to create your actual legal entity and file to obtain 501(c)(3) status with the IRS. This is a multi-step process that will involve first filing forms with your state and then, once your nonprofit organization has been created under your state's laws, filing appropriate paperwork with the IRS to earn your tax exemption. Luckily, as we discussed in Chapter 1, the IRS has recently streamlined and simplified its application process for new applicants. If you have already developed your vision and you stay organized, your new charity can be up and running in a few short months. You only need to make these up-front filings once – I will cover maintenance and other annual filings in Chapter 11.

Creating your legal entity at the state level: In order to be eligible to apply for 501(c)(3) status, you will first want to form your organization as a nonstock corporation under your state's laws. To do this, you will file Articles of Incorporation – which are like your organization's birth certificate and are sometimes called a Certificate of Incorporation – with your state's Secretary of State. Each state uses its own form for the Articles of Incorporation, and your state may have certain state-specific requirements for nonprofits. For example, as I mentioned previously, some states require a nonprofit organization to maintain a Board of Directors of a certain minimum size. A lawyer in your state who is familiar with your state's specific requirements for nonprofits will be a valuable asset to you at this early stage of the application process.

In addition, note that the IRS will require your Articles of Incorporation to include certain provisions that you will not find in a for-profit corporation's Articles, including language indicating that your organization will operate "exclusively for charitable, scientific and educational purposes" and language providing that if your organization eventually needs to dissolve, any of its remaining assets will be distributed to other registered nonprofit organizations. The lawyer who prepares your filing should understand these requirements and should be made aware of your goals for the organization.

Keep in mind that your organization's name will need to end with a corporate designation, such as "Corporation," "Corp." or "Inc." You will use the full name, including the designation at the end, every time you print or represent the name of the organization. Consistency is key from both a marketing standpoint and a compliance standpoint; remember that with every filing and step in this process, you are building a single brand and a unique, powerful identity for your charity.

Drafting bylaws: In conjunction with your Articles of Incorporation, your legal counsel will also prepare bylaws for your organization. The bylaws outline the structure of your organization in greater detail than the Articles, including by specifying the size of your Board of Directors and the names and roles of your officers (President, Secretary, and Treasurer, at minimum). They also typically describe and include the voting rights of the Board, the procedure for the election of directors and officers, the authority of the Board and the officers to act on behalf of the organization, and prohibitions against any activity or investment that would affect the tax-exempt status of the organization.

The bylaws are an important and necessary organizational document for your internal management, but you are not required to submit them to your Secretary of State. Still, you should be comfortable with the procedures and rules that they include, and you should ask the lawyer preparing them to explain any section or language that you find confusing. In the case of any future dispute among your leadership, or if you need to replace or add directors or officers at any time, you will likely need to consult the bylaws.

Conflict of Interest Policy: As a nonprofit corporation intending to apply for and maintain tax-exempt status, it is critically important that your organization prioritizes serving its charitable purpose, rather than providing (or appearing to provide) financial benefit to its directors, officers, or staff. As discussed in Chapter 4, most states allow Board members to receive reimbursement for reasonable expenses incurred in their official capacity, and the IRS permits reasonable compensation to officers and employees when that compensation is determined at arm's length – meaning that the person receiving compensation has no part in voting for, discussing or approving its amount. But keep in mind that any compensation from your organization could be subjected to IRS scrutiny, and you will need to be able to justify the spending of any funds that are not directed towards serving your charitable purpose.

The IRS strongly encourages the adoption of a conflict of interest policy, which can be drafted by the lawyer preparing your organization's formation documents. This policy will establish procedures by which any Board member or other party with the power to vote on behalf of the organization will be excluded from voting when the action being considered involves a potential financial benefit (or detriment) to that person. For example, if the organization is preparing for a fundraising event and is choosing between vendors, one of which happens to be owned by a director, the conflict of interest policy would require that this director excuse himself/herself from deliberations and voting. The policy would also require that in every instance, Board members who may have a potential conflict of interest with any voting decision of the organization share all relevant facts with the rest of the Board. As a general rule, the more informed you are about the connections and obligations of your directors and officers with respect to outside businesses and commercial interests, the more aware you will be of potential conflicts, and the easier it will be to avoid them.

The IRS provides a sample conflict of interest policy and glossary of relevant terms on its website at https://www.irs.gov/instructions/i1023/ar03.html.

Supplemental Secretary of State filings for your nonprofit corporation: Once you have officially formed your organization at the state level, you should familiarize yourself with any state-specific supplementary or annual filing requirements that you will need to make in order to keep your organization in good standing with the Secretary of State. Many states require corporations to file an annual report, which you may be able to submit yourself through an online form, along with a small filing fee; other states instead require a filing every two years. Set reminders in your calendar to ensure that you stay current with annual or biannual filing requirements, and be proactive in contacting your Secretary of State's office if you are unsure of your filing obligations.

Obtaining your organization's tax ID: Once your formational documents are filed with the Secretary of State and your nonstock corporation has begun its formal existence, your next step is to apply for a Federal Employer Identification Number ("FEIN"). Think of your FEIN as a sort of social security number for your organization – it is a unique number, issued by the federal government, that identifies the corporation for federal tax filing and reporting purposes. It may also be referred to as a Tax Identification Number, Tax ID, or simply EIN. You will need your FEIN to apply to the IRS for 501(c)(3) status, regardless of whether you plan to operate a one-person fundraising charity or a sprawling network of volunteers – in fact, you still need to obtain an FEIN even if you do not plan to hire or recruit a single employee or volunteer.

The FEIN never expires and will forever represent your organization in the eyes of the federal government. Perhaps most importantly, you will need your FEIN to open a bank account in the name of your organization, so you should apply for it as soon as your new corporation is formed. You can apply for your organization's FEIN for free online by visiting https://www.irs.gov/businesses/small-businesses-self-employed/apply-for-an-employer-identification-number-ein-online and completing a brief application. The turnaround for the application is immediate.

Applying for 501(c)(3) status with IRS Form 1023-EZ: With confirmation from your Secretary of State's office that your nonstock corporation has been created and with your newly acquired FEIN in hand, you are ready to prepare your application to the IRS for 501(c)(3) status. In the past, this step in the process presented the first major roadblock to fledgling charities: a pile of paperwork in the form of IRS Form 1023, the "Application for Recognition of Exemption Under Section 501(c)(3) of the Internal Revenue Code." Completing Form 1023, with its 31 pages of instructions, questions, schedules and requests for disclosure, was an intimidating and somewhat terrifying task; the IRS itself estimates that the average time required to complete the form and its attached schedules exceeds 100 hours.[13]

Fortunately, the IRS has recently introduced a simplified, streamlined, three-page application, Form 1023-EZ, for applicants that meet certain requirements. Most brand-new organizations seeking tax exemption will satisfy these requirements and will be permitted to use Form 1023-EZ, saving thousands of dollars and countless hours in the application process. If you are starting your first charity, you likely qualify as eligible to use 1023-EZ.

An organization wishing to bypass Form 1023 in favor of Form 1023-EZ must meet all of the following requirements, which are outlined in an "Eligibility Worksheet" published by the IRS:[14]

1. Projects annual gross receipts below $50,000 in the next three years;
2. Has not had annual gross receipts above $50,000 in any of the past three years;
3. Has total assets below $250,000, including cash, inventories, stocks, loans, land, and any other assets;
4. Was formed in the U.S.;
5. Has a U.S. mailing address;
6. Is not a successor to, or controlled by, an entity suspended for terroristic activities;

---

[13] Instructions for Form 1023 – Notices. *Internal Revenue Service.* Retrieved from https://www.irs.gov/instructions/i1023/ar02.html.
[14] Instructions for Form 1023-EZ. *Internal Revenue Service.* Rev. January 2017. Retrieved from https://www.irs.gov/pub/irs-pdf/i1023ez.pdf.

7. Has been organized as a corporation, unincorporated association, or a trust;
8. Was not formed as a for-profit entity;
9. Was not a successor to a for-profit entity;
10. Has not had its tax exemption previously revoked;
11. Is not already recognized as tax-exempt under another section of Internal Revenue Code 501(a);
12. Is not a church or a convention or association of churches;
13. Is not a school, college, or university;
14. Is not a hospital or medical research organization operating in association with a hospital;
15. Is not an agricultural research organization;
16. Is not a cooperative hospital service organization;
17. Is not a cooperative educational service organization (operated solely to provide investment services to its members);
18. Does not constitute a qualified charitable risk pool;
19. Is not organized as a supporting organization to another nonprofit;
20. Does not provide credit counseling services as a substantial purpose of its activities;
21. Does not invest 5% or more of the organization's total assets in publicly traded securities or funds;
22. Does not participate or intend to participate in loss-sharing partnerships with partners other than 501(c)(3) organizations;
23. Does not sell or intend to sell carbon credits or carbon offsets;
24. Is not a Health Maintenance Organization (HMO);
25. Is not an Accountable Care Organization (ACO);

26. Does not maintain or intend to maintain donor-advised funds;
27. Is not operated for a public safety testing purpose;
28. Is not requesting classification as a private operating foundation;
29. Is not applying for reinstatement of an exemption after revocation for failing to file required returns.

Form 1023-EZ must be filed online and requires a filing fee of $275. Rather than the three-month turnaround associated with traditional Form 1023, the IRS estimates that it will render decisions on Form 1023-EZ applications within one month. If you are not eligible to use Form 1023-EZ because your organization does not satisfy one of the above 29 requirements, I recommend that you consult professional legal counsel for assistance with filing standard Form 1023.

Information required for Form 1023-EZ: When you sit down to complete Form 1023-EZ, you will need the following information:

- The full name of your organization, including corporate designation (Inc., Corp., etc.);
- The mailing address of your organization;
- Your organization's FEIN;
- Your telephone number;
- The names, titles and mailing addresses of your officers, directors, and/or trustees (at minimum, if naming officers, your President, Secretary and Treasurer);
- Your organization's website (if available);
- Your organization's email address (if available);

- Your organization's date of incorporation with the Secretary of State.

You will be asked to certify that your organization does not participate in certain activities, including attempting to influence legislation; operating money-making gaming activities; compensating officers, directors or trustees; and providing disaster relief. If you do plan to perform these functions through your organization, know that the IRS may ask you for supplementary information related to your intentions. For example, if you plan to reasonably compensate your officers or directors, the IRS will likely follow up after your submission for an explanation as to how you will determine compensation and how you will ensure that your compensation decisions are made for your directors or officers at arm's length.

Form 1023-EZ is designed to guide you towards tax exemption with fewer obstacles in your way and may not require the use of professional legal counsel. That being said, you may wish to consult an experienced lawyer before or while preparing the form in order to ensure that you understand all instructions and answer all questions appropriately and correctly.

After you submit the application and address any follow-up questions from the IRS, you should receive your determination within several weeks. If you have satisfied the IRS's requirements, your organization will be granted 501(c)(3) status and you will have cleared a significant procedural hurdle – formerly, the most costly and time-consuming barrier to entry.

Post-exemption state registration as a public charity: The day that you receive your 501(c)(3) determination is an important one for your organization, but be aware that you will not necessarily be permitted to begin accepting charitable donations on that date. Most states require new charities to register with an agency of the state – for example, a State Charities Bureau – <u>before</u> allowing these charities to solicit any donations at all, and many states require that organizations keep their registrations current by updating them on an annual basis. Increasingly, states are allowing organizations to submit these annual filings online. Check with your state's Department of Consumer Protection, Secretary of State, or Attorney General's Office prior to receiving your 501(c)(3) determination so that you are prepared to submit the appropriate filing and are familiar with the turnaround time for your state's registration. In doing so, you can coordinate your timing so that you receive your determination from the IRS, promptly fulfill your state registration obligation, and then either mobilize your team or begin soliciting donations yourself without delay.

CHAPTER 6

VOLUNTEERS

Volunteers are a tremendous resource for nonprofits, helping organizations accomplish jobs that would not otherwise be possible due to funding or personnel shortcomings.[15] In his book *Quality Management in the Nonprofit World*, author Larry W. Kennedy notes that volunteers "supply valuable human resources which, when properly engaged, can be worth tens of thousands of dollars in conserved personnel costs to even the smallest organizations."[16] In fact, many start-up nonprofits are run entirely by volunteers and have no paid staff. Volunteers not only assist with fundraising, administrative tasks, and daily operations, but also provide an important connection between nonprofits and

---

[15] A Guidebook for Working with Volunteers, by the U.S. Fish & Wildlife Service, provides a step-by-step look at the mechanics of initiating and running a volunteer program. Techniques, alternatives, and samples are offered for use and adaptation. It is available at https://www.fws.gov/policy/volunteer_guidebook.pdf.

[16] Kennedy, L. W. (2004, March). *Quality Management in the Nonprofit World: Combining Compassion and Performance to Meet Client Needs and Improve Finances.* Reliable Man Books.

their communities and act as valuable public relations representatives.

According to the Center on Nonprofits and Philanthropy, approximately 25% of all Americans volunteer for at least one cause-related organization.[17] Volunteers have a variety of motivations including wanting to give back to their communities, supporting a cause about which they feel strongly, increasing their own self-worth, meeting new people, trying out a job, learning something new, and bolstering their resumes. Understanding these motivations will improve your recruitment efforts and help you design a successful volunteer program. As your organization matures and expands, consider appointing a volunteer coordinator to manage recruitment and to lead orientation and training programs.

Nonprofits have a responsibility to manage the time, energy, and skills of their volunteers. In his book, Kennedy states that organizations should handle volunteers in much the same way as paid employees: "Volunteers should be recruited and interviewed systematically the same way you would recruit paid staff. An orderly and professional approach to volunteer management will pay off handsomely for your organization. What you do in the recruitment phase of your work will set the standard for volunteer performance. If you

---

[17] McKeever, B. S. (2015). The Nonprofit Sector in Brief in 2015: Public Charities, Giving and Volunteering. *Urban Institute*. Retrieved from http://www.urban.org/sites/default/files/publication/72536/2000497-The-Nonprofit-Sector-in-Brief-2015-Public-Charities-Giving-and-Volunteering.pdf.

are disciplined and well organized, you will often attract more qualified volunteers."[18] Volunteers who experience this type of approach will have a much more meaningful experience and are likely to uphold this standard in their work. For this reason, this chapter discusses recruitment, screening, hiring, orientation, and training as it relates to both volunteers and paid staff members.

Before initiating the recruitment process, determine what tasks need to be done, how many people are needed to do the work, what skills are required to complete the work, and expected time commitment. It will take some trial and error before you develop a sense for exactly how many people are needed to complete certain jobs.

Recruitment: According to Rick Lynch and Steve McCurley, authors of *Essential Volunteer Management*, there are three basic types of recruitment.

1. *Warm body recruitment* is appropriate when you need large numbers of volunteers for a short period of time and the qualifications required are minimal. This type of mass recruitment is typically used to find unpaid volunteers and personnel to assist with events or short-term fundraising drives.
2. *Targeted recruitment* requires a carefully planned approach to recruit a smaller, more specialized group of people, most commonly paid employees but in

---

[18] Kennedy, L. W. (2004, March). *Quality Management in the Nonprofit World: Combining Compassion and Performance to Meet Client Needs and Improve Finances.* Reliable Man Books.

some cases volunteers as well. Most of the time, the only requirements for volunteers are enthusiasm and willingness to help, but for some projects you may need to consider physical demand, time commitment as well as professional qualifications.

- For example, suppose you are looking for someone with knowledge of accounting to help you maintain your finances. In this situation, you could target business schools, accounting firms, or finance departments of corporations.

3. *Concentric circles recruitment* requires you to target individuals who are already connected and familiar with your organization, such as friends or relatives of your current volunteers or employees or individuals in the community you are serving. This type of recruitment is applicable to both volunteers and paid employees.

To reach a broad range of candidates, utilize a variety of different platforms and strategies. Here are some of the most successful low-cost recruitment methods:

- Social media
  - o Create a page for your organization and post news and photos consistently
- Website
  - o Ensure the "Get Involved" page of your website is fun, engaging, and easy to use
- Flyers, brochures, posters

- o Get permission to post/hand out in your local library, bank, grocery store, town hall, recreation center, churches, etc.
- Newspapers and magazines
- Local television and radio talk shows
- Presentations at schools, businesses, and social clubs
- Word of mouth
  - o Ask current staff and volunteers to refer friends and family
- Volunteer matching websites such as:
  - o VolunteerMatch
  - o Idealist
  - o VolunteerSolutions
  - o Network for Good
  - o Service Leader
  - o United Way
  - o Youth Service America
  - o Points of Light

No matter which recruitment method you use, your message must be compelling. Keep it short, simple, and direct. The beginning of the message should be appealing enough to catch the reader's attention, and the body of the message should entice the reader to contact your organization for more details, or at the very least, to consider the opportunity and the work of your charity. The message should include your mission, type of work, any specific requirements for volunteers or new employees, time frame for hiring, and contact details. Explain not only the needs of the community you are helping, but why the experience will be valuable to the volunteer or employee. Here is a hypothetical volunteer recruitment message template:

SEEKING VOLUNTEERS

Have free time? Interested in supporting [organization's cause]? Consider becoming a volunteer for [organization's name].

[Organization's name] is a nonprofit organization based in [location] dedicated to [organization's mission statement].

As a volunteer, you will have the opportunity to assist with a wide variety of activities ranging from event planning to community outreach.

Volunteering is a great way to make friends, gain valuable work experience, broaden your skillset, and enhance your resume.

Our staff will provide the necessary training and equipment. All you need to do is show up with a positive and enthusiastic attitude. If you are interested in getting involved or have any questions, please email [email address], call [telephone number], or visit [website]. We look forward to hearing from you!

Whenever you refer someone to your website or instruct them to call your organization, make certain that your systems are up to the task. An interested caller or visitor should be able to quickly and easily access the information they need. First impressions count. Remember, you need these people on your team and there is often competition for the best personnel. For example, if you send someone to your website in your solicitation for volunteers, make certain your site provides all the information a prospective volunteer or employee would like to see and a way for them to express their interest. If you provide the organization's phone number in your recruitment message, make certain that the person answering calls knows how to handle personnel-related inquiries.

Screening: By utilizing different recruitment methods, your organization will hopefully attract many potential volunteers and employees. While that is a great start, some of these individuals may not be appropriate for your organization or for nonprofit work in general. That is where proper background checks come in. While some information on applicants is available publicly, to do a thorough background check, federal and state laws require that you first obtain the written consent of the applicant. Failure to obtain an applicant's written consent can result in the violation of his or her privacy rights and expose your organization to liability.

Nonprofits must conduct thorough background screening if their members work with vulnerable people. To use an extreme example, if an individual has a criminal record for child abuse, you do not want that person working at a children's hospital on behalf of your organization. Not only does this put the children at risk, but your organization could get sued for placing such an individual into a potentially improper and dangerous situation. Some states require criminal background checks for more sensitive jobs; by not conducting a thorough enough screening you may actually be violating the law.

Legal ramifications aside, remember that the most important currency your organization will trade on is its reputation in the community. You must protect your organization's reputation in all circumstances. If for any reason you lose your credibility or develop a reputation as a careless, unscrupulous, immoral or dangerous member of the community, funding will dry up and so will the involvement of key persons. You do not want one bad hire to taint your organization's reputation, so take the time to follow proper procedures when hiring, whether the candidate is a director, paid staff or a volunteer. To minimize the risks to your organization, require prospective volunteers and employees to complete job applications, submit resumes, and provide references. If these individuals are filling professional roles such as working in the finance or legal departments, verify their qualifications. Have all volunteers complete a Volunteer Service Agreement. Volunteers under the age of 18 should complete a Parental Approval Form. Check ahead of time to see if your state requires a work permit for volunteers. Before accepting any volunteers, make sure they are fully aware of any disciplinary guidelines and procedures.

Orientation: As with new leadership hires or appointments, new volunteers and employees should go through orientation programs to introduce them to the organization and their role within it. Orientation programs vary in terms of duration, structure, and level of detail, ranging from brief one-on-one discussions to highly structured sessions spanning several days. Larger nonprofits with many volunteers and employees will generally have more rigorous and extensive orientation programs than smaller nonprofits. Any orientation program, regardless of its scale, should welcome new members and express a sense of gratitude and appreciation. Information to cover during an orientation session includes:

- The mission, vision, and values statements
- Brief history of the organization
- Description of current programs
- Structure of your organization and key staff members
- Job overview and performance standards
- Disciplinary practices
- Tour of the facilities
- Training schedule
- Overview of volunteer evaluation process

By managing orientation programs in a professional manner, you are ensuring new volunteers and staff members understand your organization, what their job is, and why they are agreeing to work with you and further the organization's cause. Ultimately, you are demonstrating how valued their contributions are to the organization. Those who comprehend and recognize their positive impact on the community are more likely to remain loyal and dedicated in the future. Remember: first impressions are important, and each personnel member's orientation and introduction to the organization will set the tone for days, months and years ahead.

Training: No volunteer or staff member should be expected to fulfill their roles effectively without proper training. Nonprofit leaders often take volunteers for granted and fail to recognize the importance of training all members of the organization, not just paid employees. According to Kennedy:

> Specialized training should be designed for every person in the organization, including board members and volunteers…volunteers who are shoddily introduced into an organization's processes or who are not well managed can create chaotic inconsistency in services.[19]

The degree of training required for new personnel depends on what work new members are asked to do. An individual working as a suicide hotline operator, for example, will need much more extensive training than someone wrapping Christmas presents for children in need. Some trauma counselling centers require staff members and volunteers to undergo over 100 hours of training before ever answering a call.[20] In some cases, it may be beneficial to have a trained

[19] Kennedy, L. W. (2004, March). *Quality Management in the Nonprofit World: Combining Compassion and Performance to Meet Client Needs and Improve Finances.* Reliable Man Books.

[20] Chapter 11, Section 1. Developing a Plan for Involving Volunteers. *Community Tool Box.* Retrieved from http://www.urban.org/sites/default/files/publication/72536/2000497-The-Nonprofit-Sector-in-Brief-2015-Public-Charities-Giving-and-Volunteering.pdf.

employee work with the new member until a specialized task is learned or the relevant skillset is developed.

Delegation: Assigning specific tasks and responsibilities to personnel – the art of delegation – focuses the attention of your volunteers and employees and re-emphasizes that each individual's contributions are worthwhile. When appropriate, delegate work based on preferences and qualifications drawn from the recruitment phase. Not only will this lead to a more enjoyable experience for personnel - it will also result in a better end-product. For example, if a volunteer has a background in computer design or programming, you might ask that person to help build the organization's website. That way, the individual can develop his or her talent, feel ownership of an important project, and learn more about the organization. Consider building a database to keep track of the interests and qualifications of your volunteers and especially your employees. That way, when trying to match someone with a specific job, you can see who is best suited for it.

When you assign individuals certain responsibilities, make sure you explain the purpose of the job at hand. People tend to find tasks more meaningful if they understand the connection of the job to the organization's mission. Provide clear and concise instructions and offer written guidelines if necessary. Make sure each member feels ownership for what they are working on, either by him/herself or within a team, whether the project is large or small in scale and whatever the size of that member's contribution to it. In order for members of your organization to feel real pride in their work and a continued and strengthening connection to your mission, they should be consulted for their opinions and have the authority to make some decisions regarding their work as they fulfill their assigned responsibilities.

Evaluation: It is important to provide ongoing constructive feedback and evaluation at a level suitable to an individual's role within the organization (the evaluation process for a volunteer should be less intense than that for a board member or employee). Having evaluation procedures in place will ensure your nonprofit is considered professional and will encourage members to take their roles more seriously. An important but all too often forgotten element of the evaluation process is self-assessment, which is extremely helpful in maximizing productivity. How would members rate their own performance? What would help increase their level of satisfaction and effectiveness? Are there other projects in which they would like to be involved? Volunteers and employees should be asked to provide feedback to the organization. This feedback will help the nonprofit determine the impact of its personnel programs and policies and help improve them over time.

Appreciation: Although nonprofit work is inherently rewarding, it is always important to acknowledge the selfless commitment and contributions of your members (especially volunteers, who do not receive compensation for their efforts). You can recognize and reward hard work in several different ways, such as:

-   Saying "thank you" often (this is an obvious and easy one!)
-   Naming a volunteer / employee of the month and giving out awards for outstanding service

- Inviting volunteers to staff meetings
- Taking time to hear members' thoughts, ideas, and feedback
- Planning social events such as dinners, barbeques, or bowling
- Creating and distributing fun apparel, such as customized hats or t-shirts, which can also operate as public-facing marketing for your organization

Those who feel valued by the organization are much more likely to remain active members and may even be inspired to refer their friends and family to your organization.

As you can see, volunteers are a critical aspect of any nonprofit organization. As a start-up, you will rely on volunteers until funds come in to support a paid staff (if you wish to employ such paid employees). As your organization grows, volunteers will be essential to allow you and your employees to expand your organization's programs and reach in the most efficient manner. All the while, volunteers will represent your organization to the public and community it serves. Never underestimate their influence to shape the community's view of your organization, positively or negatively, both on the job and in their everyday lives. Free help is not always "cheap" help; if you fail to hire, manage, and motivate properly, you can be certain that your poor personnel practices will have a costly impact on your organization. Conversely, a well-implemented volunteer program can reap enormous benefits to your organization, whether you have a program of one volunteer or dozens.

CHAPTER 7

PAID STAFF

While most start-up nonprofits are volunteer-driven, some also employ staff. Deciding when to start hiring employees, how many, and for what jobs is highly dependent on the organization's needs and stage of development. Nonprofit organizations should assess personnel demands in the context of their programs, budget, and specialized needs. There are a range of different indicators that may suggest it is time to start hiring, such as: your organization needs specific expertise, your volunteers feel overworked or tired, the organization is struggling to meet its deadlines due to personnel limitations, demand for the organization's services has surged, or financial resources have increased enough for you to start paying regular salaries.

Hiring your first staff member is an exciting milestone, but it is also the beginning of a substantial long-term commitment, burdening your organization with financial and legal liabilities, expenses, and obligations such as making payroll, paying payroll taxes, providing a suitable workspace and equipment, and offering training and supervision. It is highly recommended that you consult an attorney or human resources expert to ensure you are properly handling these matters. Due to a lack of experience in both recruitment and employee management, the hiring process for start-up nonprofits can be particularly challenging for new charity founders. As a result, many organizations do not get the best out of their staff or end up hiring the wrong people to assist in getting the organization off the ground in its crucial first few months and years of operation.

Recruitment:

Job descriptions: It is imperative that jobs are filled by individuals who are willing and able to handle the work associated with their positions. Writing realistic job descriptions and listing skill requirements ensures that the right people will fill these roles. A strong advertisement should sell the job and the organization and include the position title, responsibilities, skill specifications, salary, and contact details. Keep the language simple and concise. The most effective and cost-efficient way to advertise positions is through the internet. Post the vacancy on your website and social media pages. In addition to websites such as LinkedIn or Craigslist, consider utilizing:

- www.monster.com
- www.idealistcareers.org
- www.workforgood.org
- www.simplyhired.com
- www.careerbuilder.com
- www.indeed.com

<u>Resumes:</u> Resumes are the first opportunity for candidates to make a positive impression. Inform candidates once you have received their resumes and let them know when they should expect to hear from you regarding next steps. The following qualities are important in a polished resume:

- No spelling or grammatical errors
- Cohesive, easy-to-follow story
- Relevant or interesting work experience and education
- Longevity at prior employer(s)
- Appropriate skillset

Cover letters provide additional insight into a candidate's abilities and personality. If you decide to require a cover letter, you may consider asking specific questions such as "Why are you right for this job?" and "What do you hope to learn from this role?" The more senior the position you are looking to fill, the more candidates must demonstrate leadership qualities, such as managerial skills, capacity to work with a variety of disparate personalities, and ability to navigate and resolve challenging situations using minimal resources.

<u>Interviews:</u> Once you have screened for promising candidates, start the interview process. Evaluate candidates based on standards established in the job description and look for both attitude and aptitude to do the work required. It is perfectly acceptable to refuse an applicant if you feel that the applicant is not well-suited to your program. Start each

interview by introducing yourself, your organization, and the specific position to be filled, and ask questions such as:

- How did you learn about our program?
- What interests you about working here?
- What are your strengths and weaknesses?
- What skills do you have to contribute?
- What type of work are you most interested in?
- Do you have prior nonprofit experience?
- Are you familiar with our mission statement, vision statement, and values statement? In what ways would you work towards accomplishing them?

Due to various federal laws, you must avoid questions regarding an applicant's age, sexual orientation, marital or family status, disability, religious affiliation, national origin, race, or ethnicity.[21] For more information about these laws, visit the websites for the United States Department of Labor (www.dol.gov) and the Equal Employment Opportunity Commission (www.eeoc.gov).

Onboarding: Once you have decided who you want to hire, call to congratulate the new employee and send them a letter detailing terms of employment, including start date, salary, and title. Include a line at the bottom for their signature to confirm they acknowledge these conditions. Even if your organization only has one or two employees, prepare personnel policies and procedures that outline what

---

[21] Prafder, E. W. Hiring Your First Employee. *Entrepreneur.* Accessed from https://www.entrepreneur.com/article/83774.

is expected in the workplace, ensure everyone is treated equally, and clearly state any disciplinary rules. On a most basic level, your policies should include, and you should clearly communicate to employees:

- Office hours
- Holidays
- Vacation days (two weeks of paid vacation per year is typical)
- Sick days (10 days per year is typical)
- Maternity/paternity-leave
- Employee termination policy

Every new employee must fill out a W-4 form for income tax withholding and an 1-9 form to demonstrate the employee's legal right to work in the U.S.

Compensation: While there are no specific rules for how much you should compensate nonprofit employees, the IRS can penalize the organization and/or staff member through additional taxes and fines if it deems pay to be excessive relative to the nonprofit's budget and gross revenue. While nonprofits should not excessively overpay staff members, remember that these organizations vie against each other and some for-profit businesses for the same pool of employees, so level of compensation and benefits must be competitive and fair. To attract and retain top talent, nonprofits should not rely on the altruism of their employees. In his *Legal Guide to Starting and Managing a Nonprofit Organization*, Bruce Hopkins comments:

> There is a tendency in our society to expect employees of nonprofit organizations to work for levels and types of compensation that are less than those paid to employees of for-profit organizations. Somehow, the nonprofit characteristics of the organization become transferred to the 'nonprofit' employee.[22]

When setting wages, keep important factors in mind such as average rent in your area, your organization's budget, and the types of service that employees provide. It is also helpful to review and compare salary and benefits from other similar nonprofits. Some state associations of nonprofits collect and publish salary data. Another helpful resource is www.salary. com, which allows you to search wages for various types of jobs in any geographic area for free.

Once an organization starts employing workers, it must establish a payroll system. Some states specify how frequently organizations must distribute paychecks. Check with your state department of labor about rules relating to payment frequency. If your state does not specify, you can use whatever schedule you would like (options include weekly, semi-monthly, or monthly). While some organizations handle payroll internally, I recommend working with a third-party payroll service that can aid in the process (most banks either provide or can recommend a payroll service). Payroll services are typically inexpensive and efficient. If you do decide to handle your own payroll, be sure to pay federal

[22] Hopkins, B. R. (2013). *Starting and Managing a Nonprofit Organization: A Legal Guide,* (6th ed.). Hoboken, NJ: Wiley.

and state payroll taxes on time. Check the IRS website (www.irs.gov) for more information.

The IRS discourages bonuses and commissions for nonprofit employees. In contrast with for-profit businesses, where these additional forms of payment are tied to sales, profit or as incentives to increase revenue, nonprofit employees should not monetarily benefit from the organization's fundraising performance or improvement over any given time period.

Your organization may or may not be in a position to provide health insurance to its employees. The average cost of purchasing healthcare declines as the size of your employee pool grows. If you only have one employee, for example, purchasing insurance may not make sense, but if your organization employs 20 people, you may wish to seriously consider it.

Getting the most out of your employees: Managing staff members is an extremely important yet challenging process. The most important element of managing staff is communication. It is much easier for start-up nonprofits with only a few employees to maintain strong communication than it is for larger organizations. Regardless of your organization's size, I recommend holding informal weekly team meetings either in person or over the phone to touch base and review any important information and new developments and to keep tabs on projects and programs to which employees are contributing. Make sure each employee has a work email address where they can be easily reached, and strongly encourage each employee to be responsive to messages.

In addition to providing new hires with a list of specific responsibilities and standards to ensure they understand exactly what is expected of them, it is beneficial to carry out regular assessments and appraisals, particularly in the first few months of employment. By addressing issues early on, you can spot potential problems and increase the likelihood that both you and the employee build a positive relationship and get the most out of your experience working together.

There are many ways to measure the success of your organization's employee management procedures. For start-up nonprofits with only a handful of employees, I recommend asking employees to complete employee satisfaction surveys periodically and conducting exit interviews for any employees who make the decision to leave the organization. Key indicators of success among your paid staff include low sickness and absence levels and a low rate of staff turnover.

CHAPTER 8

DIGITAL MARKETING STRATEGY

Building a website: A website is an incredibly important public relations and fundraising tool that serves as the epicenter of a nonprofit's online presence. In our digital age, it is the primary resource the public will use to learn about your nonprofit and is where most email blasts and social media posts will direct prospective donors, volunteers, and employment candidates. Nonprofit websites should be visually appealing, easy to navigate, and emotionally compelling. Ensure that your messaging is as concise and to-the-point as possible, featuring your most important content front and center and avoiding any unnecessary distractions. A cluttered website makes it difficult for users to find key information. While your messaging should be direct, it should also tap into the emotions of page visitors, inspiring them to give their time and money to your cause. I recommend starting with the following pages:

- About Us
    - o Includes your mission, vision, and values statements and any other relevant information about your organization.
- Get Involved
    - o Informs potential volunteers and employees how they may apply to the organization.
- Contact Us
    - o Includes important phone numbers and email addresses.
- Donate Now
    - o Serves as a portal for online giving.

As your organization grows, its website will likely expand to include pages such as "Projects," "News," "Blog," "Testimonials," and "Sponsors." To help you gain followers, it is also beneficial to have icons that link directly to your social media pages.

While the task of creating a website may seem intimidating, there are many companies such as Wix, Squarespace, WiredImpact, and GoDaddy that make the process relatively painless. If you are looking for one-on-one assistance, you can search for a website developer on www.volunteermatch.com or www.freelancer.com.

Importance of mobile-friendly websites: According to the Nonprofit Technology Network, approximately 30%

of today's website traffic comes from mobile devices.[23] To avoid inadvertently missing potential supporters, it is imperative that your website be compatible with tablets and smartphones and run smoothly in a wide variety of browsers and aspect ratios. In short, you need to ensure that your site is well-optimized and that it just works. You should strive for a consistent and clean look in your email blasts, as well; an organization's emails can account for a large portion of its online donations.[24] If your nonprofit uses email as a marketing tool (most do), keep in mind that many of your recipients will open your emails on their phones. When they click on the link in your email, they are going to be directed to the mobile version of your website, so it is crucial that you establish a smooth and working connection between your well-optimized site and all of your online messaging sources. Verify that the links you include in your email blasts, on your site, and in your social media profiles direct users to your intended pages and encourage your volunteers and employees to visit your website and interface with your online messaging methods to help find compatibility or user-specific issues.

Harnessing the power of social media: For many of us, checking social media has become an integral part of our daily routine. Even if you aren't an avid user yourself, many

---

[23] Why Having an Online Presence is Important for Nonprofits. *Allegiance Software*. Retrieved from http://www.allegiancesoftware. com/why-having-an-onlinepresence-is-important-for-nonprofits.

[24] Pomer, A. (2014, June). Why a Mobile Friendly Website is Important for Non-Profits. *New Media Campaigns*. Retrieved from http://www. newmediacampaigns.com/blog/why-a-mobile-friendly-website-is-important-for-non-profits.

of your supporters are spending a significant amount of their time each day on social platforms like Facebook, YouTube, Instagram, Snapchat, LinkedIn, and Twitter. According to Mediakix, a marketing agency, the average person will spend approximately five years and four months of his or her life navigating social networking sites!

As of March 2017, the top four social networks in order of monthly visitors were Facebook (1.9bn), YouTube (1bn), Instagram (700k), and Twitter (300k), and usership continues to expand rapidly.[25]

Since its launch in 2004, Facebook has become the world's largest online social network and is considered an essential marketing tool for organizations of all sizes. Given its scale and numerous options for any type of business, Facebook is the ideal starting point for your nonprofit and should be an absolute priority in your social media strategy.

YouTube is a video-sharing site that allows people to easily view, post, and comment on user-generated content. Simply by creating an account (at no cost), users are provided with a channel to which other users may subscribe, and when you upload a new video, your subscribers can choose to be notified and will automatically receive your video in their "Subscriptions" playlist. Now owned by Google, YouTube has become a massive platform for music, news and entertainment, with visitors viewing approximately six

---

[25] Kallas, P. (2017, August). Top 15 Most Popular Social Networking Sites and Apps. *DreamGrow*. Retrieved from https://www.dreamgrow.com/top-15-most-popular-social-networking-sites.

billion hours of video content every month.[26] By providing video content in addition to your text-and-picture based content, you can present a personal and human side of the nonprofit and connect with potential donors and volunteers who are more likely to be engaged by and respond to video content.

Instagram is a social media app featuring photo and video content. Owned by Facebook, the site has over 600 million users who post about a variety of subjects in their personal and professional lives, including pictures and stories relating to travel, food, lifestyle, and fashion. As Instagram has grown, corporate brands and businesses (including nonprofits) have begun to share images and video of programs and community impact.

Twitter allows its users to share text updates (up to 140 characters long), photos, videos, links and more. Like Facebook and Instagram, people can easily communicate with each other and even companies by tagging usernames in posts. This makes Twitter a great way for organizations to interact with the community directly and market themselves to people around the world. Your Twitter profile can also serve as a messaging tool to your volunteers and employees, notifying them (via public posts) of successes at each step of a new program or in the process of planning an event. By following second-hand sharing ("Retweets") of your posts and the posts of your volunteers and employees, you can see the Force Multiplier Effect in action.

---

[26] What is YouTube? *GCF Learnfree.org.* Retrieved from https://www.gcflearnfree.org/youtube/what-is-youtube/1.

Social media is becoming an increasingly powerful marketing channel for nonprofits, helping organizations tell their story, engage with the community, strengthen support, and drive results. According to Chara Odher, Senior Copywriter and part of the social team at charity: water, "Social media is designed for two-way conversation, and that's when it is most powerful."[27] Start-up nonprofits with limited marketing budgets should take advantage of social media early on since it is much cheaper than traditional advertising strategies. According to Hubspot, a marketing and sales platform, the top seven reasons nonprofits use social media are:[28]

1. Sharing news
2. Brand recognition
3. Education about the cause and mission
4. Fundraising
5. Volunteer recruitment
6. Donor recognition
7. Employee recruitment

Ask yourself which of these objectives you are trying to achieve through social networks. Every post, like, or comment should bring you closer to reaching those goals. Once you have determined what it is you hope to accomplish, decide how you will measure the results of your efforts. In-house

---

[27] Johnston, A. (2017, July 24). A Strategic Guide to Social Media for Nonprofits. *SproutSocial*. Retrieved from https://sproutsocial.com/insights/nonprofit-social-media-guide.

[28] Shattuck, S. (2017, August 2). Where Nonprofits Spend Their Time with Social Media. *HubSpot*. Retrieved from https://blog.hubspot.com/marketing/nonprofits-social-media-marketing-data.

analytics systems such as Twitter Analytics, Facebook Insights, Instagram Business Tools, YouTube Analytics break down your data and create personalized reports based on trends. While number of followers, likes, shares, and tags can be a good indicator of brand awareness, there are other more complex metrics that are just as important. Examples include: [29]

- Tracking online sentiment surrounding your brand through Mention, Meltwater, SocialMention, and Google Alerts.
- Determining how many social interactions it takes before one of your prospects becomes a donor through Marketo and Convertro.
- Tracking the number of searches for your organization and comparing this data against other similar organizations through Google Insights and Google Trends.
- Analyzing how frequently your social media platforms drive traffic to your website through Google Analytics.

In addition to the above, websites such as Sprout Social, Radian6, TrueSocialMetrics, and Bit.ly are great resources for personalized data analytics. Remember to be patient with your results. Nothing worthwhile happens overnight. If used properly, these insight tools will enable you to finetune your social media strategy to achieve the best outcome in the long-run. According to Bridgett Colling,

---

[29] The Complete Guide to Non-Profit Social Media. *Canva*. Retrieved from https://designschool.canva.com/blog/social-media-for-nonprofits.

See3 Communications' Director of Content Strategy, "It's important to set reasonable expectations and know that social media and content marketing is a long game. You're not going to put one post out there and instantly get hundreds of dollars in donations. Like any good relationship, it's all about communication over time."[30] Be persistent; plan your content in advance and post on all of your channels regularly, even daily or multiple times per day, in order to improve your exposure and stay in the News Feeds of users who are likely to interact with you online.

Designing social media pages: When designing social media profiles for your organization, reflect on your nonprofit's goals and how these platforms are going to help you reach them. For inspiration and benchmarking purposes, analyze the social media pages of similar organizations and industry leaders. Which ones have gained the most traction and why? Which qualities can you emulate and how can you avoid their mishaps?

Most social networks have business accounts for organizations. For example, you can create a Facebook page, enroll in the YouTube nonprofit program, or create a business profile on Pinterest. These accounts typically come with built-in data analytics features. As discussed previously, these features are incredibly useful tools.

---

[30] Johnston, A. (2017, July 24). A Strategic Guide to Social Media for Nonprofits. *SproutSocial*. Retrieved from https://sproutsocial.com/insights/nonprofit-social-media-guide.

The basic content of your social pages must at a minimum include your logo, a description of what your nonprofit does, and your organization's contact information. Ensure you post regularly and are responsive to any comments, inquiries, or posts mentioning your organization. For start-up nonprofits with limited time and resources, I suggest focusing on 1-2 platforms only. It is better to have a strong presence on a few platforms than to be inactive and unresponsive on multiple, which may damage your reputation more than not having a social media presence at all.

Maintaining social media pages: While social media is typically less formal than other marketing platforms, you must use good judgment to ensure your posts remain professional and appropriate. Avoid taking any political stances – especially as this may implicate the IRS's rules against political advocacy for all tax-exempt entities – and be absolutely sure to keep your organization's profile entirely separate from your personal account. Require that your volunteers and employees do the same.

According to Steven Shattuck at HubSpot, the posts of nonprofits with the most successful social media presence follow a three-part system, which he refers to as the "three A's":[31]

- Appreciation: 1/3 of your posts should recognize your supporters, volunteers, and donors.

---

[31] Lee, K. (2015, June 16). Social Media for Non-Profits: High-Impact Tips and the Best Free Tools. https://blog.bufferapp.com/social-media-non-profits.

- o Spotlight key volunteers and donors. The people you feature will likely share these posts on their own pages, which will improve your visibility.
- Advocacy: 1/3 of your posts should share the content of other groups or nonprofits.
  - o Like, retweet, share, or comment on fellow nonprofits' posts. This helps with community building and boosts your visibility to their followers, plus it will encourage these other groups to like and share your content.
- Appeals: 1/3 of your posts should solicit donations or help.
  - o Share success stories to demonstrate your organization's impact.
  - o Consider starting a crowdfunding campaign (see next chapter on fundraising for more details).

Engage your audience by asking questions and starting interesting conversations. Photos and videos typically attract more "likes" and views than plain text, so keep your posts varied and interesting.

Use hashtags to attract page visitors and to help you find and join relevant conversations. Hashtags consist of a word or group of words not separated by spaces after the # sign such as #marketing, #buylocal, #photooftheday, or #flashbackFriday. While it may seem like a silly trend, the reality is that hashtags can greatly expand the reach of your posts, attract followers with similar interests, and help you scope out the competitive landscape. You can even create your own brand hashtag unique to your organization – a short slogan or an abbreviation of your organization's title, to be used by you and your supporters in posts about your efforts.

CHAPTER 9

FUNDRAISING

Just like for-profit businesses, nonprofit organizations need money to function and achieve their goals. This is where fundraising comes in. Fundraising is the process of soliciting donations on behalf of a cause and is the lifeblood of the nonprofit industry. As discussed earlier, contributions made to 501(c)(3) organizations provide income tax deductions for donors – an important incentive for both individuals and corporations to continue their charitable giving. Unfortunately, many new nonprofits do not invest enough time developing thoughtful fundraising plans and strategies. By applying strategies used by for-profit businesses, nonprofits are more likely to secure the relationships and support they need to sustain themselves in the long-run. Before initiating your fundraising campaign, ensure you have a strategic plan in place to guide your efforts. A basic plan should include your organization's fundraising goal, a list of potential supporters, and the fundraising methods you plan to use.

Fundraising goal: Your fundraising goals should follow the S.M.A.R.T criteria (discussed at length in Chapter 3) and, at a minimum, be enough to cover your organization's campaign costs. While contributions are typically received in the form of money, your nonprofit may benefit from donated equipment and other resources. Decide what your organization needs most and include this in your fundraising plan. In addition to mapping out how much money you intend to raise, you must clearly define what specific outcomes you anticipate resulting from each program or service. These results should be quantifiable and publicly evident to clearly demonstrate the potential success of your efforts.

Sources:

Friends and family: The ideal fundraising campaign seeks money from a diverse pool of prospective donors. As with for-profit start-ups, most funding for new nonprofits comes from its founders, board members, volunteers, friends, and family. While you may feel awkward asking friends and family for money, they are arguably the greatest resource for seed funding as they are the most likely to have faith in your organization before it has really taken off.

Board and board contacts: Even if your board does not consist of wealthy individuals, all members should be expected to donate to your campaign. Potential supporters will likely want to know if you have 100% board participation before contributing their own money. In addition to their own contributions, board members should create a comprehensive list of other potential sources based on their personal and professional networks. Examples of connections include business partners, fellow club members, and neighbors. Once this list is finalized, board members should reach out to these contacts personally for support.

Cause-related contacts: Once you have exhausted your and your board's personal networks, target people who care about the cause your organization represents. For example, if your nonprofit raises money to rescue animals, potential donors might include individuals who have taken in rescue dogs from the local animal shelter. If your organization provides veteran services, you may speak to a local family who have been affected by a family member's combat deployment in Afghanistan or injuries sustained during service.

For the purpose of establishing reasonable goals and budgeting, estimate to the best of your ability how much each of your prospects is likely to give. While this task is easier said than done, research to find any information on prospective donors' charitable giving history. It is best to remain conservative in your estimations.

While you may be tempted to spend seed money to cover start-up costs, the primary use should be to demonstrate your organization's ability to deliver results. By proving to early donors that your programs can have the desired impact, you will find it easier to raise additional funding in the future. Start small and be realistic. Demonstrate that you can put money to use in a way that has an immediate impact. Grow from there.

<u>Grants and corporate giving:</u> As your organization moves beyond its initial fundraising efforts, you may also solicit grants and corporate donations. Grants are contributions typically made by foundations and government agencies. Program grants support specific programs or projects while general operating grants support organizations as a whole. Grants can be an important financial resource for nonprofits, and if you have the time and resources available, it may be worth researching grants for which your organization may be eligible and investing time in completing applications and speaking to representatives of various foundations regarding the procedure for reviewing applications and making decisions. However, keep in mind that grants may not be the ideal starting point for all start-up organizations. According to PolarisGrantsCentral, "grants are a double-edged sword. While the simple fact is that they are free money to complete a set task, one must understand that there is a big difference between free money and easy money."[32] In addition to grants being highly competitive and having specific eligibility parameters that exclude many nonprofits (especially start-ups), other issues include:

- Preparing grant proposals requires tedious planning, research, and work.
- The grant approval (or rejection) process is usually slow.

---

[32] Advantages and Disadvantages of Government Grants. *PolarisGrants Central*. Retrieved from <u>http://www.polarisgrantscentral.net/instruction. htm.</u>

- Most grants are on a reimbursement system, requiring nonprofits to spend money upfront (to be reimbursed later).
- Organizations are required to spend the grant money according to complex regulations and laws. You may need to hire a professional (such as an accountant or attorney) to understand and navigate these parameters, which costs money.

If your organization does decide to pursue a grant, locally-based family foundations are the best place to start. Unlike their larger "name-brand" counterparts, these small to mid-sized organizations tend to keep a low profile and are therefore not as easy to find. Many local foundations restrict grants to nonprofits with which they are personally familiar, so start networking within your community to find opportunities. Research who is giving grants to organizations similar to yours and introduce yourself. Your proposal submission should not be the first time a foundation hears from you. Once you have built relationships with and received support from local foundations, you will have the credibility to qualify for funding from larger-scale regional and national players.

Another important resource to consider are corporate social responsibility (abbreviated as "CSR") programs. CSR can take many forms, including grants, matching gifts, volunteers, event support, or marketing partnerships. Through matching gifts programs, companies match their employees' donations, creating a powerful Force Multiplier Effect that not only increases the size of each donation but incentivizes donors to give more. By researching your supporters' employers, you may find fundraising opportunities through matching gifts and other CSR initiatives.

Case statement: A case statement, also known as a case for support, is the primary tool nonprofits use to fundraise. It is a short, professional, and persuasive document that compels readers to support an organization. The most important step in writing this statement is capturing the essence of your nonprofit's identity, which should resound clearly and strongly throughout your campaign. What does your organization represent and why should people be passionate about supporting you? A great way to emotionally connect with and inspire your audience is by leveraging the power of storytelling. Through a narrative, you can show potential supporters what they can be a part of and how your organization has made a difference in the past.[33] This is particularly important for start-up nonprofits, which lack the resources to invest in more formal marketing campaigns. Georgetown University's Center for Social Impact Communication conducted a survey among 81 nonprofits in the Washington, DC area to gain insight into the way nonprofits perceive the effectiveness of narratives. 96% of participants agreed that storytelling is an important aspect of their organizations' communications and 75% reported spending less than 5% of their annual budgets on

[33] Chase, V. (2015, March 17). 5 Things (Almost) Everyone Gets Wrong about Nonprofit Storytelling. *EveryAction*. Retrieved from https://blog.everyaction.com/guest-post-5-things-almost-everyone-gets-wrong-about-storytelling.

storytelling.[34] While there is no "correct" recipe for a case statement, the basic framework should include:

- Your nonprofit's mission, vision, and values
- The history of the organization
- Current programs and services
    - o Measurements of success
    - o Ongoing requirements to keep these services running
- Evidence demonstrating past success
    - o Testimonials from those you have helped
        - Include relevant photographs that depict the heart of your mission
    - o Data
        - Where appropriate, utilize charts that help readers digest the information
- Funding needs and giving options for potential donors

Methods: There is a certain amount of anxiety that goes along with asking someone for money. Luckily, advancements in communication technology have made seeking donations and maintaining relationships easier and more effective than ever before. While there is a long list of ways to connect with supporters, the following are some of the most effective:

---

[34] Stories Worth Telling: A Guide to Strategic and Sustainable Nonprofit Storytelling. *Meyer Foundation*. Retrieved from http://www.meyerfoundation.org/how-we-work/strategies/stories-worth-telling.

Email: Email has become one of the most important fundraising tools of the modern era. The first step is to create an email account for your nonprofit so that you can send personalized messages, mass updates, or digital newsletters to your distribution list (which will grow over time). When appropriate, tailor your content to the individual as much as possible to show donors that their generosity is valued by your organization. Ensure your emails are formatted professionally and in a mobile-friendly way and always provide a link to your social media platforms and website. In every email, make sure to clearly direct readers to your online donation options.

Note: While the traditional method of direct mail can be effective for more established organizations, it is not recommended for start-up nonprofits. This method is one of the more expensive options and is difficult to scale without a direct-mail consultant.

Face-to-face interaction: This can range from standing on the street with a donation bucket to networking with members of the community who may have interest in your cause. Consider handing out pamphlets, brochures, or flyers about your organization and its mission. In addition, one-on-one interactions are a great way to secure larger donations. If possible, the member of your organization who knows the potential donor should lead the one-on-one interaction. To be clear, this should be a planned and expected meeting, not an unannounced knock at the door.

Special events: Hosting a fundraising event is a fantastic way to raise money and awareness, but this method can be expensive and demand a significant amount of personnel. For these reasons, plan carefully and stick to a strict budget. Low-cost event ideas include cocktail parties hosted at a board member's house, bake sales, online auctions, and athletic events. Remember, since events cost money, you must make sure you are raising more than you are spending. During the planning stage, I recommend asking friends and family how much they intend to give so you can gauge your budget.

Social media: As discussed at length previously, it is becoming increasingly important for nonprofits to have a strong social media presence. Post updates and fundraising goals on your organization's social pages, and in order to fully benefit from the network effect, ensure these updates can be easily shared by your supporters.

Crowdfunding: Web services such as Kickstarter, Indiegogo, GoFundMe, and Crowdrise provide special online platforms that help nonprofits publicize their needs, collect contributions, and acknowledge key supporters.

Phone calls: Cold call potential donors to introduce yourself and the organization, explain your fundraising goal, and gauge their interest. For special programs and initiatives, consider calling key contacts and large donors to personally ask them for their help.

Stay organized: No matter what methods you decide to utilize, keep your efforts highly organized by creating a spreadsheet that tracks your organization's donor interactions. Include columns for contact information, donation history, future giving capacity, last time your organization reached out, and other relevant notes. More established nonprofits with hundreds of contacts may decide to use an electronic database system to manage and track donor interactions. This kind of software is called customer relationship management (abbreviated as "CRM"). Popular CRM companies include: Salesforce, SugarCRM, and CivicCRM. A few platforms that are specific to nonprofits include: DonorPerfect, DonorSnap, and GiftWorks. While CRM systems can increase your record-keeping efficiency, they are not necessary for start-up nonprofits with fewer contacts. Furthermore, monthly fees and necessity for technologically-trained staff to manage the programs will add to your cost basis.

Say thank you: To complete the cycle of fundraising outreach, show appreciation for the donors who have kept your organization up and running. Through sincere and personalized interaction, your organization will form strong and lasting relationships, making a strong case for continued giving and ensuring future financial stability. Here are some suggested ways to demonstrate your gratitude:

- <u>Make a phone call:</u> After receiving a significant contribution, call the donor as soon as possible to express your gratitude and explain how their donation will be utilized to make a difference.
- <u>Send a handwritten note:</u> While it may seem cheesy, a handwritten thank you note demonstrates thoughtfulness and serves as a lasting reminder of how valued the donor's support is.

- <u>Write a social media post:</u> Recognizing donors through your organization's social media platforms is a great way to make supporters feel special and appreciated.
- <u>Write a newsletter:</u> By including real stories and testimonials, a newsletter can be a powerful way to illustrate how vital your donors' support is for the work you do. Highlight individual donor contributions (with their permission).

Respect donor anonymity, if requested: One final note on ethical fundraising and responsibility: in the course of your solicitation of donations, you may find that some donors request anonymity and ask that you not publicize or disclose their identity and/or the amount of their donation(s) to your organization. For your records and in order to satisfy IRS record-keeping requirements, you must keep an internal record of the donor and the amount donated, but in order to maintain your organization's integrity, you must also respect a donor's request for anonymity and keep the requested information limited to your highest level of leadership on a need-to-know basis. This may seem counter to the principle that your organization should strive to be as transparent as possible, but for the purposes of fundraising, you should respect the wishes of your donors and reassure them that you are taking measures to safeguard their privacy if asked to do so. Keep records of donations for which anonymity is requested protected under lock and key if necessary – but of course, include the anonymous donation in your budgeting and financial records and report it to the IRS if audited and when filing returns.

CHAPTER 10

ADMINISTRATION AND GOVERNANCE

Once your tax-exempt organization is up and running, your solid foundation of leadership and strong brand identity will assist you in your recruiting, fundraising and management efforts. Equally important, however, will be the steps you take to maintain your organization's tax-exempt status and to satisfy your continuing obligations to the IRS. Failure to do so would undo all of your hard work and planning, so you must be sure to stay current with annual filings, keep detailed financial records, and maintain transparency and accountability policies.

The flow of information: As we have discussed, the key to success for any charity is a clear understanding among its leaders and volunteers as to how best to serve the organization's charitable purpose. This is the reason we prioritize developing a business plan, budgeting, and holding quarterly board meetings – the IRS itself suggests in its commentary that a well-organized and focused charity is more likely to obey tax laws, effectively serve charitable interests, and avoid scrutiny.[35] Your organization should regularly review its mission statement and tailor each quarter's planned activities and goals toward furthering it. Your internal messaging to staff and volunteers should reflect your focus and the ways in which each person and activity will bring your charity closer to fulfilling its purpose. These are more than simply motivational practices – certain annual tax filings (covered in this chapter) will require you to describe your mission. For this reason, your mission should guide your recruiting and marketing, and you should educate your personnel at all levels, highlighting your successes and addressing weaknesses and shortcomings in the charity's operation.

Be direct and transparent with your internal messaging. Never assume that because your charity serves a noble cause, its supporters and staff will maintain an unwavering passion. Rather, keep the people at every level of your organization engaged by frequently broadcasting the ways in which your organization is making a difference in its community or impacting its target demographic, and keep the Force Multiplier Effect in mind when you do.

Enthusiasm and passion are contagious – people will appreciate transparency and will feel valued when you share positive news with them. You can maintain morale and keep your staff focused simply through persistent messaging.

---

[35] Governance and Related Topics – 501(c)(3) Organizations. *Internal Revenue Service*. (2008, February 4). Retrieved from https://www.irs.gov/pub/irs-tege/governance practices.pdf.

Maintaining your organizational documents and ensuring long-term compliance: You may not feel the need to revisit or revise your Articles of Incorporation, Bylaws, or Conflict of Interest Policy once your organization is operational, especially because those foundational documents will likely remain unchanged for years and will operate in the background of your organization (except in the case of a conflict or dispute). Still, because tax law can change without much warning, you should consult an attorney familiar with the laws governing 501(c)(3) organizations at least every couple of years to ask about any new or revised IRS or state requirements for nonprofits and to ensure that you are not required to modify or add to any organizational document that governs your charity. If you have had to consult your Conflict of Interest Policy, it is especially important that you understand and are applying its terms correctly.

The rest of your organization's leadership should also have access to your formational documents. There is no reason to keep these materials under lock and key – a strong baseline understanding of how your organization was formed and how it is to be managed is critical for your leadership, both when recruiting board members and once your board is well-established. Per the IRS's own commentary, an active and informed board is more likely to run a compliant organization.

The importance of an independent board: I previously covered the advantages and disadvantages of maintaining a large board and the benefits of establishing committees (executive, advisory) and delegating responsibilities. Regardless of the size of your board, keep in mind that a governing board should – as much as possible – be made up of independent individuals rather than individuals with shared relationships, whether in previous or current business dealings or by virtue of family ties. In the event of an audit, the IRS will review the composition of the board to assess the potential for conflicts of interest and misuse of funds by board members. A board composed of independent and unrelated members will suggest that no subgroup or collection of board members is inclined to work against the best interests of the organization to pursue other interests, and that no board members are being unfairly influenced or coerced into voting for or against any action to be taken by the organization.

In the case of large organizations, the IRS will also review if the charity has given control to a management company or other individuals outside of the Board of Directors, which will invite scrutiny into those decisions and those managing entities. If an organization has local chapters or affiliates, the IRS encourages the adoption of procedures and policies from the top down that promote consistency between the parent organization and its various offices and branches.

Management policies: The IRS does not require charitable organizations to implement specific governance or management policies, but in the case of an audit, its guidance suggests that it will request and review any policies relating to conflicts of interest, executive compensation, fundraising, document destruction, whistleblower claims, and governance decision-making.[36]

---

[36] Ibid.

Executive compensation: Because a charity may only provide reasonable compensation to officers, directors and key employees, your organization should be prepared to report the process it uses to determine compensation (if you do compensate any members of leadership) and to justify that compensation by truthfully reporting that you rely on review, deliberation and approval of compensation packages by independent individuals and incorporate comparability data into those individuals' decision-making. In order to be prepared for this kind of inquiry, even if you do not develop a written compensation policy, keep detailed minutes and records of any meetings, discussions, or decisions made regarding compensation, and always remember that scrutinizing 501(c)(3) executive compensation is a priority and large area of focus for the IRS.

Keep in mind that compensating executives or employees introduces employment tax issues for both the organization and the compensated individuals. A 501(c)(3) nonprofit is not required to pay federal unemployment taxes on employee wages, but for each employee paid $100 or more in wages in a calendar year, the nonprofit must withhold and deposit federal income tax, Social Security and Medicare taxes from wages and pay its share of such taxes to the federal government. The organization should have a Form W-4 on file for each such employee and should provide these employees with Form W-2 for filing. I will discuss these tax filings in more detail in the next chapter.

Conflict of Interest Policy review: Though the IRS does not require nonprofits to adopt a written Conflict of Interest Policy, most organizations voluntarily do so at their formation in order to promote board member independence and to establish a procedure for addressing conflicts. The IRS encourages regular evaluation of this policy – annually or biannually, you should add a review of the policy to your board meeting agenda as a discussion and action item, and if you ever need to consult or act on the policy, you should adhere to its procedure consistently so that no two conflicts are addressed differently.

To stay informed and on top of potential conflicts, I recommend requiring your directors, officers and all employees in leadership positions to disclose any financial interest that such person (or a relative) has in any business entity that is considering entering into a contract or providing services to the organization at any time.

Fundraising and record-keeping: Your charity's fundraising solicitation materials are required by federal law and the laws of most states to be accurate, truthful, and candid. You may not mislead potential donors or misrepresent actions your organization has taken, actions that you plan to take, or the scope and structure of your organization and its charitable efforts. Take care to be specific and accurate when telling donors how the organization plans to utilize donations. Voluntarily disclose your organization's recent activities and use truthful and specific descriptions of those activities. Be upfront with donors about the timing of the charity's anticipated future efforts and use of funds. If you are soliciting donations for disaster relief, for example, remember that you are addressing a time-sensitive and urgent need for funds; donors likely expect that their money will be put to use quickly.

Critically: keep a record of every single donation that your charity receives, issue receipts to donors, keep receipts from purchases, and be prepared to share all of your records with the IRS or state regulators in the event of an audit. Monitor your funds received and expenditures closely – this will allow you to compare your actual finances to your budget and make adjustments to both on an ongoing basis. Further, it will allow you to keep references to fundraising figures accurate and up to date in your marketing. Avoid claiming that "100%" of donations will support your charitable cause or relief effort (unless it's true). In at least some states, this can be interpreted to be misleading, as most charities will at least need to deal with administrative costs.

When your charity needs to make a payment or transfer funds, the IRS requires that you record the following information for your records:

- <u>If Paying by Check:</u> check number; amount of donation; payee's name; date the check amount was posted
- <u>By Electronic Funds Transfer:</u> amount transferred; payee's name; date the transfer was posted
- <u>By Credit Card:</u> amount charged; payee's name; transaction date[37]

Never commit to spending resources or taking action if you will not be able to do so. In business, your credibility

---

[37] Compliance Guide for 501(c)(3) Public Charities. Prepared by the IRS Tax Exempt and Government Entities Exempt Organizations Division. Retrieved from https://www.irs.gov/pub/irs-pdf/p4221pc.pdf.

is vitally important to your success; in running a charity, the inability to act upon promises or representations to donors will endanger your entire organization and its tax-exempt status. In contrast, establishing realistic goals and accomplishing them as a team raises the morale and profile of your entire organization. Make sure that your staff and volunteers understand this point, and consider adopting training procedures or solicitation guidelines to coordinate responsible and truthful fundraising appeals. Establish a system of oversight to monitor and approve solicitation materials that accurately reflect your mission and scope, and at the same time, monitor your marketing to ensure that exaggerated or inaccurate materials do not reach the public.

Keeping minutes at board meetings: Beyond financial record-keeping, you should make sure that the details and minutes of board meetings and voting results are recorded during each meeting and kept organized in a minute book. In the event of an audit or regulatory scrutiny, a full roadmap of your organization's decision-making will prove that policies and activities were deliberated, voted upon, and approved as required by your bylaws and without undue influence.

You should encourage board members to review the organization's financial statements and should address the organization's finances at every board meeting. If the board believes for any reason that it should rely on an independent auditor or expert to review the finances, the board should consider and vote on this action.

Retaining and disposing of documents: In today's digital age, the secure, reliable storage of electronic data and the responsible handling of files and media have become principal business concerns. In order to prevent a catastrophic loss of electronic records, be sure to implement and adhere to consistent backup policies and maintain multiple copies of your fundraising and administrative records. To safeguard the privacy of your donors and staff, consider implementing a privacy policy that will password protect your organization's records, using a secure server for file storage, and prohibiting the transfer of records outside of your organization or outside of your offices.

If you use paper records, store them in locked filing cabinets overnight or when not in use and consider adopting a policy for scanning their contents in order to create electronic backup copies. Keep copies of invoices received and payments made on behalf of the organization, including copies of checks – in short, you want to create and maintain a paper trail that would justify and represent every dollar entering and leaving the charity.

If your organization handles Protected Health Information or has access to patient records or the personal health details of any individuals for any reason, note that you will have certain privacy and data security responsibilities under HIPAA. In that instance, I recommend reaching out to a healthcare attorney to discuss your record-keeping and to ensure that you understand your obligations under HIPAA.

The IRS reports that an organization must retain receipt and expenditure records for federal tax purposes for a minimum of three years. Employment tax records should be maintained for a minimum of four years. Organizational documents (such as the bylaws) should be maintained permanently.

Ethical concerns, complaints, and whistleblower policies: Given its preferential tax treatment, a 501(c)(3) organization is held to a high ethical standard by the federal government and is expected to promote the public good and prioritize its charitable function above all else. As you might imagine, not all such organizations live up to this expectation – as with any beneficial arrangement with the government, abuse and improprieties can occur within the 501(c)(3) scheme. Accordingly, the IRS encourages the Board of Directors to adopt policies for receiving and addressing employee complaints and to allow for employee reporting of suspected improprieties or misuse of resources. In the event of an audit, the IRS may investigate whether insiders or staff members diverted or misused assets of the charity, and it may ask whether leadership was aware of such misconduct and has adopted a written complaint or whistleblower policy. The flow of information is key here, as with all governance issues; if you can prevent or resolve improprieties early and discover them yourself rather than waiting for the IRS to discover them, you can get ahead of troublesome misconduct before it snowballs into a debilitating scandal.

CHAPTER 11

ANNUAL FILINGS

With principled and responsible governance, your 501(c)(3) public charity will have a strong foundation and a roadmap for future growth from day one, assuming you can appeal to donors and volunteers consistently and continue to address a public need effectively. Once you have momentum and have been operating for months, it can be tempting to focus exclusively on day-to-day operations and consider your formational paperwork and registration requirements to be behind you. It is logical that you want to keep moving forward and focus squarely on helping the public and growing your entity. However, note that you will need to stay current with your annual state and federal public and tax filings – failing to do so for three years will eliminate your tax exemption and undo all of your other hard work.

Annual state filings: corporate reports; maintaining charity registration: To remain in good standing with your state, recall that you must file an annual report with your Secretary of State, which occurs either annually or every two years (depending on the state). This filing typically involves a small fee, but it is important to stay current – in most cases, you can submit the filing yourself, often online, and you do not need to consult a lawyer for assistance.

On an annual basis, you will also need to update your registration with your state's charities bureau, Department of Consumer Protection, Attorney General's Office, or whatever agency governs charities in your state. This will allow you to continue soliciting donations and operating as a recognized charity, so set a recurring reminder in your calendar and be sure to understand your state's requirements well in advance of your charity's one-year anniversary.

Employment filings and withholdings: Note that if you plan to utilize paid employees, you will need to register your organization with your state's Department of Labor before making your first hiring. I recommend that you consult your state's agency or an attorney licensed in your state to understand the implications of bringing on paid staff and satisfying both state and federal employment law obligations. Generally, if you have hired employees, your tax-exempt organization will be responsible for federal, state and local employment taxes, and as an employer, your organization must withhold federal income tax and Social Security and Medicare taxes from employees' wages.[38]

Meals, lodging, clothing, and similar services provided to employees for their well-being are subject to Social Security

---

[38] Exempt Organizations: What Are Employment Taxes? *Internal Revenue Service*. Retrieved from https://www.irs.gov/charities-non-profits/exempt-organizations-what-are-employment-taxes.

and Medicare taxes, just like wages paid in cash, but note that meals provided for the employer's convenience and on the employer's premises are not taxable, and note that lodging is not taxable if offered on the employer's premises and as a condition of employment.

Traditional employers (i.e. non-charities) are required by law to report and pay federal unemployment tax, but fortunately, 501(c)(3) organizations are exempt from federal unemployment tax requirements.[39]

Annual federal filings: Forms 990, 990-EZ, and 990-N: Public charities are required by federal law to file an annual tax return using Form 990 ("Return of Organization Exempt from Income Tax") or one of its two variants, Form 990-EZ ("Short Form Return of Organization Exempt from Income Tax") or Form 990-N ("Electronic Notice for Tax-Exempt Organizations Not Required to File Form 990 or 990-EZ"). The type of Form 990 that you are required to file is based on your charity's gross receipts and total assets, and it is due midway through the fifth month following your organization's annual accounting period (in most cases, this due date will be May 15).

The determination breaks down as follows:

- Charities with gross receipts normally less than $50,000 will file Form 990-N.

---

[39] Ibid.

- Charities with gross receipts between $50,000 and $200,000 and total assets below $500,000 will file Form 990-EZ or Form 990.
- Charities with gross receipts above $200,000 or total assets above $500,000 will file Form 990.

Form 990-N (e-Postcard): Traditionally, an accountant or tax specialist would assist a large organization of the kind that would be required to file a full Form 990. As the organizer of a new charity, you will likely be able to file Form 990-N, which is also called an "e-Postcard" and which requires only the following eight pieces of information:

- Your entity's FEIN (Tax ID Number);
- The tax year start and end date (often, Jan. 1 and Dec. 31);
- Legal name and mailing address of the organization;
- Any other names the organization uses;
- Name and address of a principal officer;
- Web site address, if the organization has one;
- A statement that the organization's annual gross receipts are $50,000 or less; and
- If applicable, a statement that the organization has terminated or is terminating.

Form 990-N does not require you to submit a budget or financial records – but of course, remember that the IRS can audit your organization at any time, ask to review all of your records, and eliminate your tax exemption if you have been deficient in your record-keeping. Still, if you are eligible to use Form 990-N, you will be able to complete and submit it in mere minutes. The form is provided online only and includes a User Guide and a Frequently Asked Questions page to address any specific concerns you may have.[40]

Form 990-EZ: If your organization receives gross receipts above $50,000 but below $200,000, you will need to file Form 990-EZ instead. Like IRS Form 1023-EZ, this "EZ" form was introduced as a short-form alternative to the intimidating and overwhelming standard Form 990. Besides basic identifying information about your organization, the form requests:

- A breakdown of revenue, expenses, and changes in assets, including in asking for donation totals, investment income, gross income from certain types of events, expenses from fundraising, money from grants, compensation paid to members, professional fees and expenses (i.e. rent, utilities, printing, postage);
- Balance Sheet totals, including cash, savings and investments, the value of land and buildings owned, and asset totals;
- Details regarding the organization's three largest program service accomplishments, including a

---

[40] Annual Electronic Filing Requirement for Small Exempt Organizations – Form 990-N (e-Postcard). *Internal Revenue Service*. Retrieved from https://www.irs.gov/charities-non-profits/annualelectronic-filing-requirement-for-small-exempt-organizations-form-990-n-e-postcard.

description of services provided and the number of persons benefited;

- A list of officers, directors, trustees and key employees, including average hours per week devoted to position and reportable compensation and benefits;
- Employee and independent contractor compensation details; and
- Miscellaneous information regarding changes to governing documents, unrelated business income, political expenditures, loans to members, and the organization's accounting methods.

Assuming that you kept complete and accurate records of monies collected and spent, you should be able to complete this form, but I recommend consulting a tax specialist or attorney in order to ensure that you complete it correctly and understand what information the IRS requires.

Form 990: In the event that you are required to prepare and submit a full Form 990 – because your organization is collecting annual gross receipts in excess of $200,000 or has assets greater than $500,000 in value – you will want to consult a tax specialist and your attorney to facilitate this process. The form requires information related to every part of your income, expenses, assets, employees, goals, and activities, including a detailed accounting, and it asks about 40+ potential attachments, some of which may apply to your organization (and some of which will not). I recommend finding a local accountant or other tax specialist who prepares these forms for large organizations in your state – and be prepared to turn over reams of well-organized financial bookkeeping.

Stay on top of annual filings: If your passion for charitable work stems from harnessing boots-on-the-ground enthusiasm and organizing creative and effective events to bring about change in your community, it can be easy to lose sight of behind-the-scenes paperwork like the Form 990 and annual state requirements. Remember that every piece of the puzzle is integral to your success, however – and educate your fellow leaders and volunteers on the importance of the nuts and bolts of running your organization.

CHAPTER 12

RESTRICTIONS AND PITFALLS

A 501(c)(3) organization runs the risk of jeopardizing its tax-exempt status if its directors and officers are unaware of the restrictions imposed on its activities by the IRS. Some of these restrictions may seem obvious, but it is important that you internalize them and communicate them to your leadership and even your employees. If you have additional questions regarding the tax implications of any of the information in this book, I advise that you consult a tax specialist or your attorney with your specific facts and to better understand your state's rules.

Prohibition against private benefit: As we previously discussed, your organization's goal of serving a specific charitable purpose must always be your top priority. The question of what purpose your charity serves is the principal concern of the IRS in the application for exemption process, and in maintaining your charity and its tax-exempt status, you should always ask yourself what charitable benefit is introduced, sustained or expanded by each action that you take. In the case of an audit, the IRS will investigate whether your organization's finances and votes reflect the fulfillment of the charitable purpose you reported on your application – this is why record-keeping (financial and donation records; meeting minutes; payroll; marketing materials) is so important. Besides distributing donations or providing direct aid to your target demographic, you will likely have certain expenses, which may include event organizing costs and staff compensation. You must always be able to show that your expenses further your charitable purpose and are not lining your pockets or unreasonably compensating the members of your organization.[41]

Public charities are permitted to provide only an insubstantial, incidental economic benefit to anyone who has a private interest in the organization and holds a position where he or she can influence the organization's decision-making (i.e. an officer, director, or key employee). Your charity may not be structured, and may not implement any rule or policy, to direct any portion of the charity's income or assets to such an "insider" on a percentage-of-revenue basis, and the value of any economic benefit provided to such a person cannot exceed the value of the services they have provided. Because the value of board membership and leadership is difficult to determine, the majority of nonprofit board positions are unpaid. Any payment to an insider of your organization that could be interpreted as being greater than the exact value of a specific service could be considered to be an "excess benefit transaction" by the IRS; these types

[41] Compliance Guide for 501(c)(3) Public Charities. Publication 4221-PC (Rev. 7-2014). *Department of the Treasury, Internal Revenue Service.* Retrieved from https://www.irs.gov/pub/irs-pdf/p4221pc.pdf.

of transactions introduce excise taxes on the insider and will endanger your tax-exempt status. Further, board members are never permitted to vote or deliberate on any monies that they will receive, which prevents you from introducing blanket compensation for the entire board.

I recommend that you clearly communicate to prospective board members and officers that involvement with your charity is unpaid. Your leadership's passion for your cause and willingness to contribute should be the motivating factor for anyone who joins your organization, rather than a desire to supplement employment or make money during off-hours and weekends. You may reimburse members of the organization for costs incurred – for example, if someone purchases office or signage materials in a pinch, while organizing an event – but always keep in mind the fact that no member of your organization should be receiving any of your organization's money for their own private benefit. Your donors trust you to responsibly utilize donation funds and turn their individual acts of generosity into a force-multiplied movement or support effort – use your infrastructure and resources to maximize the public benefit, which will keep you in the good graces of the IRS and will allow you to further your mission on a daily basis!

Political campaign involvement/opposition: According to the IRS, public charities are absolutely prohibited from directly or indirectly participating or intervening in any political campaign involving a candidate for public office. This restriction prohibits using donations to either give money to a campaign or create an opposition effort or protest – after all, specific rules outside of the 501(c)(3) scheme exist that govern campaign financing and political action committees. Violating this restriction may result in the revocation of your tax-exempt status. Your organization may be full of like-minded, politically inclined volunteers, but a charity is not a super PAC and must never act like one.

This does not mean that 501(c)(3) organizations are absolutely prohibited from any activity related to politics. A charity may conduct voter education campaigns and may set up voter registration and get-out-the-vote efforts – if and only if those activities are performed in a non-partisan manner. This can introduce a tricky tightrope – how do you ensure that your volunteers are not overstepping the non-partisan line and either preaching to or attempting to influence would-be voters? Again, this is where communication with members of your organization and volunteers at all levels is key. You must stress to each volunteer involved that any attempt to praise one candidate over another or speak negatively about a particular candidate while serving the public at an event is absolutely prohibited and would be devastating to your organization. You should adopt a review process for any and all written materials or signage that will be presented to the public, and if you ever feel the need to make a political statement of any kind within your organization, you should make it very clear that your view does not represent the views of the organization.[42]

Remember: your organization is non-partisan. Its members may have strong political opinions and leanings, but these

---

[42] Ibid.

biases and preferences should not reach the eyes and ears of the public through your tax-exempt charity. If volunteers wish to make a difference for their preferred political cause, they should volunteer for a PAC or a campaign.

What about public policy concerns?: If your charity addresses an issue that is not strictly political but has become politically charged in the modern news media and politics – for example: prisoners' rights, women's healthcare and safety, or veterans support – you may be wondering how the restriction on political campaign involvement affects your organization, or what its limits are. The IRS permits 501(c)(3) charities to take positions on public policy issues, including issues that divide candidates for public office, but it does prohibit any issue advocacy that qualifies as political campaign involvement under a multi-factor test. In short, charities may not, in their messaging:

- Identify one or more candidates for a given public office;
- Express approval or disapproval for one or more candidates' positions and/or actions;
- Make politically charged statements close in time to an election;
- Reference voting or the election itself when discussing an advocacy issue;
- Focus on an issue in a way that distinguishes one particular candidate, especially if that candidate is well-known as having a particular opinion similar or contrary to the organization's message; or

- Create any public-facing political communication that it would not have put forth if not for an imminent election.[43]

The last point is the lynchpin here – it is generally advisable that your organization, regardless of its proximity to a political issue, avoid adjusting its messaging in any way during and because of election season (local, state, and/or federal). Refrain from mentioning the election in your materials, encourage your volunteers and staff not to refer to the election in public forums or in preparing any materials or efforts, and try not to think of election season as an opportunity for increased fund-raising or issue awareness. Stay consistent in your message and remember that your charity's goals are no more or less important during or outside of an election cycle. Consistent public need should be consistently addressed.

Legislative activities and lobbying: For reasons similar to those justifying the prohibition on political campaign involvement, public charities may not engage in what the IRS could determine to be substantial lobbying – though they are not absolutely prohibited from involvement.

What constitutes "substantial" lobbying? According to the IRS, lobbying efforts are substantial for an organization with expenditures of less than $500,000 per year if the organization spends more than 20% of its expenditures on lobbying efforts. At the $1,000,000 and $1,500,000 marks, the percentage changes. Any amount above this nontaxable

---

[43] Ibid.

ceiling will introduce a 25% excise tax on money spent and may endanger the tax-exempt status of an organization if this limit is exceeded in four consecutive years.[44]

Besides lobbying efforts, the IRS permits organizations to make non-partisan analysis, study or research available to members and the public, and it permits communication with members to keep them informed of proposed legislation of direct interest to the organization and its members. This includes local, state, and federal legislation.

Avoiding record-keeping deficiencies; stay current with filings: We have repeatedly discussed the need for thorough and accurate record-keeping throughout this book, but I feel that I should reiterate the importance of this most basic requirement as a final point. Once your organization is operational, you may feel that there is not enough time in the day to manage your messaging, respond to all donor and volunteer inquiries, and keep track of your finances. No matter the circumstances, whether you are gearing up for an enormous fundraising event or managing daily staff concerns and juggling personalities within your organization, you must in every single instance keep a record of every dollar you collect, every dollar you spend, and every decision being made by the organization – without exception. If the IRS audits you or requests information or documentation, they will not make exceptions for donations collected during a hectic period or look the other way regarding unjustified

---

[44] 26 USC § 4911 – Tax on Excess Expenditures to Influence Legislation.

expenditures that occurred because you were confused by the sometimes-arcane Internal Revenue Code.

Strong record-keeping will reflect well on your charity and will allow you to stay on top of your financial health and the viability of growth efforts or fundraising events. Poor record-keeping will likely cost you your tax-exempt status. It's that simple. Be vigilant with your staff – establish clear policies for providing receipts and be sure to enforce them – and utilize regular compliance checks. Better to recognize and resolve an issue immediately than months or years later, during an audit.

The importance of insurance: With so many moving parts and so many restrictions to avoid and requirements to fulfill, I'm sure you recognize by now that keeping your charity afloat and moving forward will involve a great deal of effort and your reliance on a number of other people. A public charity is more than an ideal or the noble cause it serves; it is a corporation, nonprofit but in all other ways a business, and you will need to adopt and maintain a business executive's attitude and way of thinking in order to succeed. You will also need to protect your entity from unfortunate eventualities in every way possible, and that includes obtaining an appropriate level of insurance for the corporation.

Many insurers offer insurance packages to nonprofits that include general liability insurance, property insurance, professional liability insurance, auto insurance, crime insurance, employee benefit insurance, sexual misconduct insurance, and a number of other types of coverage. If you have a staff of employees or volunteers working in a fixed office location, you should speak with a broker about coverage for your business and its office facility, and you should ensure that all staff and volunteers are covered by the policy. A broker will be able to address your specific needs – for example, if you or a member of your staff uses a car or larger vehicle to travel for fundraising or to events, your policy should include auto insurance.

You should also inquire with your broker about directors and officers liability insurance, which protects your nonprofit's decisionmakers from claims by employees related to wrongful termination, harassment, discrimination, and other intentional actions taken by your board or the charity's officers. This insurance can also cover your board and officers in the event of a breach of contract claim that is made against them personally, for example, by a vendor – but be sure to understand the limits of a policy before you sign on the dotted line, and be sure to compare quotes from several insurers. Some policies may not carry a deductible; some insurers may offer annual assessments of your employment practices; some policies may require you to pay costs as incurred rather than up front. Understand what your specific nonprofit will require, then make a decision in conjunction with your board and educate your entire leadership as to what policies you have put into place.

As always, communication is critical. Talk to your broker, talk to your accountant, and share all information with your organization's leadership. Make sure everyone is on the same page, and do so as early as you can.

CHAPTER 13

NEXT STEPS AND COLLECTED RESOURCES

If you have followed the structure of this book chapter-by-chapter and used it as a guide at each stage, you may have the bulk of the formational work and early stages of running your organization behind you. If so: congratulations! You are well on your way to success, and I hope that you will consult previous chapters for tips and strategies on maintaining your tax exemption and running an effective organization. If you instead read through the entire book for a more complete understanding of what tasks and challenges you will face and are now preparing to take your very first steps, I hope that you feel well-prepared and encouraged to join the ever-increasing ranks of nonprofit organizers and generous Americans seeking to improve their communities and serve others by forming new public charities and utilizing the benefits of Section 501(c)(3). Now is the perfect time to explore forming your own nonprofit, and because so many books, blogs, and websites have been published and posted on topics ranging from formation to management,

I hope you will supplement your reading of this book with additional advice from other resources.

Official IRS Guidance: In addition to publishing lengthy and in-depth commentary on rules governing 501(c)(3) tax exemption, the IRS also maintains several websites tailored specifically to new and upstart charity organizers that I found to be very useful while forming my two charities and writing this book. At www.irs.gov/charities-non-profits/charitable-organizations, the IRS has compiled guidance on exemption requirements, applications, required filings, restrictions, employment, state-specific instructions, and web-based courses for visitors interested in learning about (or looking to confirm) the rules and obligations of starting and maintaining a 501(c)(3). The IRS also publishes extensive user-friendly guidance on its "IRS Stay Exempt" website, www.stayexempt.irs.gov, which it has designed for visitors of all levels of expertise and at all stages of 501(c)(3) formation and management (including those just "Starting Out" and "Existing Organizations"). The Stay Exempt site also contains a Resource Library with links to webinars, frequently asked questions, a model "Life Cycle of an Exempt Organization," and podcasts. As the number of tax-exempt organizations continues to grow, the IRS continues to expand its knowledge base for organizers and directors of new 501(c)(3)s, and the materials published and freely accessible on the IRS's various sites will often provide answers to any procedural or tax-related question you may have, in addition to providing general advice on responsible administration and governance.

Foundation grants: Whether you are looking at grants as a source of possible funding while starting your 501(c)(3) or are the director of an established organization looking to expand your funding sources by applying for a grant, www. grants.gov should be on your list of resources to consult in order to explore your eligibility and learn more about available government funding. As I mentioned in Chapter 9, local foundations and grant opportunities may provide a more realistic source of grant money than competitive private national or government foundations, but when looking into grant options, every resource is useful. To that point, a number of websites have been formed to aggregate grant options, including www.grantwatch.com, www. grantspace.org, and the Center for Nonprofit Excellence's grant opportunities page at www.thecne.org/engage/grants. Individual institutions also maintain their own websites to promote their grant programs, including United Way, Farm Aid, and Humanities New York, to name just a few.

Private online resources: As the nonprofit sector continues its recent boom, you will discover an increasing number of private blogs and websites devoted to assisting you in forming and maintaining your organization. Websites such as those maintained by the National Council of Nonprofits (www.councilofnonprofits.org), the Society for Nonprofits (www.snpo.org), Charity Navigator (www.charitynavigator. org) and state-specific foundations publish free resources that you will likely find useful at any stage of starting or managing your 501(c)(3), and private blogs and articles intended to inform nonprofit directors and officers are published online daily in increasing number.

As we have discussed, the process of organizing a nonprofit and effectively managing it requires conviction, dedication, passion, and a strong understanding of the rules and challenges associated with each step of your journey. My goal in writing this book was to combine my experience and observations with lessons I have learned from a variety of resources, including strategies from books and blogs on nonprofit management and official guidance from the IRS – it will be up to you to put this collected information into practice and to create something lasting, personally fulfilling, and beneficial to society and those less fortunate than you. The fact that you began reading this book in the first place suggests that you are passionate about improving the world around you. Continue to embrace new ideas and stay motivated and you will find success in all of your efforts going forward.